FROM KOSHER TO HALAL

*When greed, politics and the sneaky destruction of
Western Civilization intertwine*

Translated from French by David Smith

Suzanne Bousquet

Contents

FOREWORD TO THE ENGLISH EDITION

The average American and Canadian spends much of their time filling the role of "consumer", shopping for products their entire lives to meet necessary sustenance as well as frivolous luxuries. Many enjoy comforts and convenience thanks to the supermarket and its broad offering of packaged goods. But few consumers realize the extent that religious certifications have played in the vast industry that supplies those supermarkets, even though the practice of religious intervention into our food has existed for nearly one century.

The business of kosher certification has certainly been mysterious or unknown to the majority of consumers, regardless that newspapers have occasionally written promoting it. And in the few isolated challenges to this practice, such as the 1954 speech by a prominent member of the Daughters of the American Revolution, Marian Strack, the newspapers and religious representatives have united to squash any dissenting critique without permitting ample public debate. Today, any consumer that probes into the pertinent details of the religious certification business is met with suspicious secrecy or vague, obscuring responses - perhaps a strategy that sustains and grows this controversial practice.

The typical consumer may think "big deal, since I don't notice this is going on, it must not be affecting my shopping very much". And that is the surprising paradox: awareness versus dominance! As of this 2019 writing, the world's largest kosher certification agency, OU Kosher (Union of Orthodox Jewish Congregations), claims to be supervising over one million products globally. And this is just one of over 4500 different entities that perform these services. Kosher certification is so predominant in packaged goods that there are numerous categories where consumers simply will not find brands "free" from kosher certification, for instance flour, sugar, oatmeal, coffee and aluminum foil found in most markets. Pick up a case of bottled water, even nature's glacial spring water from the pristine mountains of Whistler, Canada, and odds are in favor that it is certified kosher!

Short articles and amateur videos eventually propagated the media of the twenty-first century, attempting to alert consumers to the kosher certification that dominates their kitchens. Nothing noteworthy was put out into the public mainstream until 2010. That was when Sue Fishkoff wrote *Kosher Nation - Why More and More of America's Food Answers to a Higher Authority*. Now the title of this book made it clear that America's food supply was becoming dominated by the tiny kosher seals that most consumers miss. But given that the author, Ms. Fishkoff, was a prominent advocate for Jews and Judaism, it was even more clear that the book's theme was apologetic in favor of the religious enterprise that has insidiously seeped into our secular retail markets. Nevertheless a thorough reading of the book still revealed several nuggets portraying the realities of an industry, realities that many critically-thinking consumers might not find, shall we say, "kosher". Such was the example highlighted where a business owner who was threatened to lose the kosher certification of his ice cream plant finds that this issue will effectively result in his product being removed from the supermarket distribution chain. This was revealing!

Ms. Fishkoff was provided access to key players in the kosher business, and *Kosher Nation* provided deep insight to the layperson unfamiliar with Kashrus (the kosher dietary laws of Judaism). However, there was still much to be learned for the broad consumer population of America.

In 2017 a small California company published an app, KosChertified? Grocery List +, which jumped at the opportunity to make kosher awareness an inclusive matter for all consumers to understand. It offered a database of products NOT Kosher-Certified (NKC), grocery list functionality, a brief kosher certification education and other resources all available for the smart phone user. The concept of presenting NKC products served a practical solution for consumers of both camps: kosher-keepers could use this information to avoid products found in the app, and consumers who weren't following religious dietary laws or objected to religious intervention of their products could construct digital grocery lists from the relatively few items still free from ubiquitous kosher certification.

The company promoted the KosChertified? app in various media platforms, and numerous videos were produced to help. But after about one year, a solid record of positive reviews, and a video with over 10,000 views, the app gained attention from entities that would smear it and have it deplatformed. Apple was the first to remove the useful tool from its iTunes App Store, followed shortly by YouTube's removal of all its kosher education videos for consumers. While numerous apps exist to this day on Apple iPhones that are produced by kosher agencies for kosher keepers, the one kosher app created outside the Jewish community and for all the people, regardless of faith and identity, was not permitted to exist and compete in the capitalist free market. Given the advantages of the KosChertified? app over its competition (for instance the speed in discerning that a product is NOT Kosher-Certified), it would not be surprising that the entire deplatforming was a business tactic in itself. Then again, given the one-sidedness of newspaper reporting on religious certification, there may be an agenda in play, and KosChertified? might have been a spoiler to the approved narrative.

Regardless of the letdown, an honest effort was still pursued by KosChertified? to evoke broad public interest in this food-related industry, and they still continue to produce attention-getting information such as professional surveys indicating that 1) 90% of savvy American shoppers cannot recognize the most common kosher seal in America and 2) only 1.5% recognized the COR kosher seal (a Canadian kosher agency) found on a popular big box store's dishwashing detergent. Their 500 respondent survey indicated that 39% prefer to not have any religious intervention in the production of their food products, and so maybe the food and kitchen product companies realize that having bold transparency on such a business practice might not fly well. That might explain why recent consumer research found that kosher seals measured just one tenth the size of all other (non-religious) certification seals found on the same product packaging. Is this just a deceptive trade practice meant to keep broad kosher awareness on the "down low"? Just take a break after reading the first chapter of this book and peruse www.TheKosherQuestion.com, where you'll find *A Quantitative Study of Kosher Certification: Kosher Seals and Public Awareness*. You may be surprised.

The end product of three years of writing and investigation, the present book about kosher and halal is the first of its kind written from outside the Jewish and Muslim communities. Scribed in French by Canadian Suzanne

Bousquet (*Du cachère au halal: Quand cupidité, politique et sournoise destruction de la civilisation occidentale s'entremêlent*), this comprehensive book also provides an in depth examination of religious slaughter of animals for food consumption. You'll discover the passion Ms. Bousquet has for both animals and our precious European-based democracies as she delivers the counter-argument to Ms. Fishkoff's *Kosher Nation* and other newspaper propaganda in favor of religious certification.

American consumers put their trust in several federal agencies that have oversight on our food production and product labeling: U.S. Department of Agriculture (USDA), the U.S. Food and Drug Administration (FDA), and the Federal Trade Commission at a minimum. And while Ms. Bousquet's book focuses on the Canadian government agencies that decide on these similar regulations, the issues presented here are pertinent to all Western nations! For most of these nations have separated Church and State from government matters, while guarding the religious freedom in their citizens' lives. But what occurs behind the politician's and agency's closed doors might be something far from the liberal democratic ideals that have been fought for. In both the United States and Canada, we find a progressive liberalism that is not only pulling, but accelerating to the left in matters of "human rights". While at the same time there is a religious fundamentalist movement that is pulling further and stronger from the right as it imposes its culture, its will and ancient particularism on the secular norms of society, possibly disrespecting "animal rights". And this leaves the vast majority of citizens - detached from political activism, yearning to live unbothered, but caring for both human and animal rights - in the middle of this dichotomy, powerless and threatened to lose it all. There is a battleground right now using food and religious certifications as a means to an end. Who could have foreseen this one hundred years ago, and have our leaders let us down?

If you're an American parent reading this, ask yourselves why your child's milk carton served in the school lunch program is almost certainly kosher-certified, even after religion was litigiously yanked out of the public schools of a Christian-founded nation long ago? Or why there is no choice for students to have one offered that is NOT Kosher-Certified? Or why the leading kosher agency in the world is politically advocating for tax payer-subsidized kosher and halal meals for students at public schools? Or why the religious non-profit umbrella group for which the same kosher agency belongs was advocating in their "Resolutions" for the release of the notorious convicted spy Jonathan Pollard? Is that the kind of political lobbying you, consumer, have been unwittingly paying for all these years simply because you were not "kosher aware"?

For everyone reading this, when you see a NON GMO, Gluten-Free, Vegan, Fair Trade or USDA Organic label, ask yourselves why these certification seals are ten times larger than the kosher seals that are usually segregated from all the others on the product label? Which of these certification seals are truly used for "marketing"? And why, when you see a list of textual attributes on a package, you'll probably never read "KOSHER" or "KOSHER CERTIFIED", even when there's a small kosher seal on the front corner?

These are just a few of the questions that most people will never tackle, because most in the U.S. and Canada have not been brought into kosher or halal awareness. You won't find TV or magazine ads boasting about the religious certification of a product (but you will for the non-religious certifications), and the meat you buy at the supermarket likely will not indicate that it was religiously slaughtered, even if it was. If you hadn't read this book, you may even feel that there's no need to be concerned about the normal routine for procuring sustenance, for life is pretty good! "My interests are being cared for, and modern life is treating me well!" Or is it?

You may not care for the business of food, religion and politics. But rest assured, it is reaching out for you. As a citizen with "consumer rights", you just may find new purpose in your daily life, one where you can actually make a difference having been woken to the realities so vividly detailed in Ms. Bousquet's magnum opus.

Eric Sieger
Consumer Rights Advocate at www.TheKosherQuestion.com
January, 2020

INTRODUCTION

Why This Book Was Written

This book seeks to fill a remarkable gap, viz., the absence from any Canadian publisher's catalogue of any rigorous explanation of the business of kosher and halal certification from an outsider's point of view. This absence can be explained in several ways, including a certain sensitivity about dealing with a subject whose mere mention causes controversy—as if there were domains that must remain taboo from the mere fact of their religious connotations.

No question should be dodged in a democratic society worthy of the name. And yet... that practices so directly affecting consumers are treated with so much discretion is striking, especially in this era of "enlightened" consumerism. A relatively recent legal field, consumers' rights continue to evolve and establish a body of jurisprudence from which the following four major principles emerge:

1. Transparency, or the availability of all information by which consumers can make enlightened choices.
2. Accountability, or the responsibility of merchants toward their customers.
3. Traceability, meaning the ability to know the source and exact nature of products.
4. Social acceptability, meaning that a practice may be considered reprehensible by public opinion.

The protection of the law in this regard covers everyone (civic equality). The laws regulate commercial practice and provide, if appropriate, for penalties. In Quebec, the Law on Consumer Protection plays this now-essential role. "Merchant" is defined under this law as follows: A person who professionally carries out commercial acts, i.e., principally transactions of goods or services.

1

The agencies which sell religious certification services and companies which profit from products labelled kosher or halal fit these criteria. Consequently, their activities should constitute an object of study; their intrinsic religious character should not render off-limits a close examination of their practices. Hence the present book. Without claiming to be exhaustive, it modestly puts down a first milestone toward a better understanding of a reality unknown to the public. I hope it may inspire other researchers to study the subject further.

What This Book Is Not

The present book is in no way an accusation against the religions known as Judaism or Islam, nor does it seek to ostracize any group or individual. Abstracting from any sorts of particularism or communitarianism, it is no speech for the prosecution or appeal for intolerance. In this sense, it is neither a catch-all nor an escape valve.

This book does not, then, question the freedom to practice a religion, a right inscribed in the Canadian Charter of Rights and Freedoms. It neither accuses nor promotes any religion in particular, nor its opposite, atheism. Nor should one seek here any condemnation of dietary practices based on religious precepts. That is not its purpose.

Since in Canada the majority of purchasers do not belong to any of the relevant religious denominations, and since there are disagreements within these organizations themselves about the norms to be maintained, it is legitimate to inquire publicly about the well-foundedness of such standards. This is not a problem which arises in the case of organic certification (e.g., by Ecocert Canada, Québec Vrai, or the Organic Crop Improvement Association), a label considered among the most carefully regulated in North America, based upon rational principles and with an impressive rulebook, and not upon particular and arbitrary beliefs.

The decision to choose an organic product rests entirely with the consumer (willing to accept, if necessary, a higher price), whereas most articles offered at the grocer's (and therefore unavoidable in practice) include a so-called religious certification as part of a package deal. The universality of this practice and its integration into the commercial process, along with easily imagined pressures on producers anxious to get their products onto grocers' shelves, have come to violate the freedom of conscience recognized by the Canadian and Quebec Charters.

2

Those Ubiquitous Little Kosher Seals Nobody Notices

The great majority of consumers do not even seem to notice them, and yet there are discreet kosher logos on nearly 80% of products at the grocery. And subtle pressures are increasingly felt by producers to acquire halal certification as well. These two labels are not publicized; they remain a mystery for many people. And meat from animals slaughtered in kosher or halal fashion are still not subject to systematic, strict identification and labeling even now, as we shall see later in this book.

Then there is the issue of certification costs and their global impact on companies and consumer prices. The destination and actual use made of the money received via kosher and halal certification have not been exposed to the light of day. This opacity is very different from what is displayed on cash receipts, invoices, package labeling, and newspaper fliers, which clearly indicate the portion of the cost born by consumers: percentages and total amounts of provincial and federal taxes, environmental costs (electronic equipment, computers, televisions), environmental taxes (tires), amounts donated from each purchase made in the context of charitable campaigns supported by participating merchants or producers, etc.

If Current Trends Continue...

The use of the concepts kosher and halal as marketing tools is an invention of the 20th Century. Originally applying to meat, they are now found on an increasingly broad range of food and household products, pharmaceuticals and even cosmetics. In constant expansion since the globalization of the economy, the market for certified products is increasingly active in trying to satisfy the most radical practitioners (i.e., the "fundamentalists") of the religions involved. And this is precisely what is disturbing, insofar as it involves a simultaneous resurgence of so-called religious rules in public places.

This accelerating intrusion of the religious sphere into the public commercial sphere has not drawn the attention it deserves. Worse, our governments have integrated the industries of the kosher and halal markets into our economy while considering them merely one sector of (profitable) activity among others. The consequences of this laissez-faire, notably its threat to social cohesion and the rights of women (impossible to dissociate

3

from a social project centered on the separation between political and religious power), have not yet been measured.

History shows us that in the absence of clearly maintained landmarks, the instrumentalization of religion for occupying the terrain of politics returns like a boomerang again and again. States are always torn between advances and retreats, the price of movement being a break with the status quo. And one of the State's mandates as guardian of the "common good" is to regulate industries and protect consumers against possible abuse or fraud.

May this book enlighten the reader on the high stakes that can be glimpsed behind apparently innocent practices (or practices presented as such) in the essential domain of human consumption, and furnish a few reference points and possible paths toward a solution.

NOTE

All examples and cases cited in this book in order to analyze the subject come from serious sources in the public domain, viz.: material from the web, official corporate websites or sites recognized by the certification agencies and businesses involved themselves, journalistic reports and radio and television broadcasts connected with these bodies, registers, data, communiqués and studies by governmental institutions or provincial and federal ministries, articles, theses and reports by researchers, professors or university chairs, inquiries or polls by private firms, reference works and, of course, the packages of numerous grocery products. There was little choice but to rely on these sources. Particular public personalities, institutions and companies (moral persons) are mentioned by name. But declarations and statements by the concerned parties are cited only in connection with the facts and words attributed to them by the above-mentioned sources, where we know the persons concerned have expressed themselves publicly or formally responded to one or more questions concerning them. "They cannot consider this work defamatory except in the etymological sense, i.e., of qualifying something as not glorious."[1]

Critical intellectual activity need not be subordinated to the discipline of regional law. If certain interested parties feel themselves implicated by the content of this book, that is above all because they are involved to various degrees in monopolistic religious certification procedures and commercial practices supported by power apparatuses to the detriment of the most elementary consumers' rights. May the present work enlighten them on this subject.

CHAPTER ONE

FROM KASHRUTH TO KOSHER INDUSTRY

A diet more than three thousand years old, kashruth is a collection of alimentary rules observed by believing Jews, especially orthodox and conservative. Its source is in the Bible, and it is an integral part of the history of the Israelite people—and thus of Jewish identity. After the flood, God promises never to destroy the world and makes a covenant with Noah. He dictates several fundamental laws to which humanity must conform. Among them is not to eat the flesh of a living animal (sic).

Then, 1275 years before Christ, on Mount Sinai, God (Yahweh) gives his Law to Moses. It figures in the first five books of the Bible (the Pentateuch). Within Judaism, this work is called the Torah (Law). In exchange for obedience to this Law, the Jewish people in exile will be protected and earn themselves a country. The prohibitions found there form the basis of kashruth. The "chosen people" distinguish themselves in particular by the way they eat.

Rabbis have delivered their own interpretations of the Law collected in the Talmud. A true civil code covering all aspects of Jewish life, the Talmud contains the Mishnah (a commentary on the Torah), consisting of oral traditions put into writing between 180 and 220 AD by Rabbi Yehudah Hanasi, and the Gemara, a commentary on the Mishnah, 4th-6th Centuries.

Rabbi Yossef Caro (1488-1575) specifies the laws of kashruth in his treatise Shulchan Aruch (lit., "The Set Table"). This codification of Talmudic jurisprudence is completed by the notes and additions of the HaMappa (lit., "Tablecloth") of his contemporary Rabbi Moses Isserles.

The treatise Chullin in the Talmud (2nd-3rd Century) describes the technique of ritual slaughter of animals, called *shehita*. It is forbidden to eat mammals and birds which have died naturally or been slaughtered in a manner incompliant with ritual (Deuteronomy 14: 21, Exodus 22: 30). Whoever violates this prohibition must purify himself (Leviticus 17: 15 and 22: 8; Ezekiel 4: 14).

Rabbi David Bar-Hayim of the Merkaz HaRav Yeshiva confirms in a study that Judaism establishes a distinction between individuals based on religion.[2] Meat designated "kosher," and by extension the absolute obligation that the slaughter be carried out only by a believing Jew, comes from a conception which figures in the Hebrew Law (the *halakha*), whereby non-Jews (*goyim*) are considered animals. The terrestrial soul of non-Jews has the same type of anima as that of impure animals (such as pigs or apes); the goyim are creatures judged very inferior, and this is why meat from an animal slaughtered by them cannot be kosher.[3]

In the same way, a food product or other necessary product can only be "kosher" under rabbinic supervision. This principle introduces a clear distinction between the pure (Jews) and the impure (non-Jews) into the very heart of our industrial processes. As regards wine, even if the grape per se is kosher, it is the production process which allows a wine to bear this label.[4] The equipment and machinery must only enter into contact with kosher products. Only kosher ingredients are used, including the proteins employed to clarify and stabilize the wine.

A pious orthodox Jew (observant of the Sabbath) must be involved at every step: harvesting the grape, pressing, fermenting, and bottling.[5] There have been seizures of cases of illegally imported kosher wine in Montreal, in both the Outremont and Côte-des-Neiges neighborhoods, in recent years. In the latter case, the kosher wine came from Israel.[6]

Wine prepared by non-Jews is called *stam yainom*.

An "Irrational" Dietary Regime

The practice of Judaism rests on the observance of precise divine commandments called *mitsvot*. The Talmud lists 613 of these concerning man's duties to God, his neighbor, and himself. Eating kosher is part of the duties toward God. Kashruth belongs to the category of *mitsvot* called *chukim*, rules the reasons for which are beyond human understanding.

8

Coming from divine decrees, this dietary regime whose purpose cannot be made clear must be followed simply because it is commanded.

Essential Rules of Kashruth

Permitted foods are described as kosher, while those consider unfit for consumption are called *treif*. The main fundamentals of kashruth are:

1. The choice of animals and the method of ritual slaughter;
2. The prohibition against consuming blood, the sciatic nerve or suet;
3. The prohibition against mixing meat and milk products.

Concerning land mammals: "These are the living things which you may eat among all the beasts that are on the earth. Whatever parts the hoof and is cloven-footed and chews the cud, among the animals, you may eat. Nevertheless, among those that chew the cud or part the hoof, you shall not eat these: the camel, because it chews the cud but does not part the hoof, is unclean to you. And the rock badger because it chews the cud but does not part the hoof, is unclean to you. And the hare, because it chews the cud but does not part the hoof, is unclean to you. And the swine, because it parts the hoof and is cloven-footed but does not chew the cud, is unclean to you." (Leviticus 11: 2-7).[7]

The giraffe, although kosher, is omitted because its consumption poses technical problems: it is not known how high up the neck to cut during ritual slaughter.[8] Dietary prohibitions apply to any mammal not possessing either of these traits: 1) Ruminant 2) Cloven-hoofed.

Why these criteria? Rumination is said to symbolize the condition of the student who must constantly assimilate the teachings of the Torah. Cloven hoof? They represent the need always to distinguish good from evil so as not to distance oneself from God...

Birds

The Torah does not give criteria for permitted birds but cites forbidden species, which includes their eggs:

And these you shall have in abomination among the birds, they shall not be eaten, they are an abomination: the eagle, the vulture, the osprey, the

9

kite, the falcon according to its kind, every raven according to its kind, the ostrich, the night-hawk, the sea gull, the hawk according to its kind, the owl, the cormorant, the ibis, the water hen, the pelican, the carrion vulture, the stork, the heron according to its kind, the hoopoe, and the bat. (Leviticus 11: 13-19)

The Talmud later established norms for which birds are permitted (Babylonian Talmud, treatise Chullin 65a 1882):
The presence of a crop, a sort of diverticulum of the esophagus before it enters the thoracic cage. Food remains there a certain time to soften;
The presence of a gizzard whose mucous internal membrane is easily detached from the musculature (found in non-carnivores and granivores);
The existence of a supplementary claw or spur. Clean: domestic fowl such as the chicken, goose, duck, turkey, partridge, quail, pigeon, guinea fowl. Unclean: wild birds/birds of prey, ostrich, pheasant, etc. The pheasant is permitted in the German Jewish community.

Aquatic Animals

These you may eat, of all that are in the waters. Everything in the waters that has fins and scales, whether in the seas or in the rivers, you may eat. But anything in the seas or the rivers that has not fins and scales, of the swarming creatures in the waters and of the living creatures that are in the waters, is an abomination to you. (Leviticus 11: 9-10)

Permitted fish: haddock, anchovy, pike, cod, trout, sole, perch, smelt, halibut, pollock, haring, mackerel, sardine, salmon, tuna, etc. Forbidden fish: shark, ray, monkfish, eel, lamprey, turbot, sturgeon (including roe), catfish, swordfish, wolfish, etc.
The swordfish raises questions. Sephardic Jews allow it while British Ashkenazim forbid it. The treatise Shulchan Aruch lists criteria for permitted fish (beyond scales and fins): the presence of a vertebral column; scales, even small ones visible in the light; swim bladder pointed on one end and smooth on the other. Fish do not have to be ritually slaughtered and must only be taken alive from the water.
All mollusks, crustaceans and other salt water and fresh water invertebrates are forbidden: shrimp, lobster, crayfish, spiny lobster, sea urchin, oyster, scallop, mussel, squid, octopus, sea turtle, etc.

Other Animals: Worms, Insects, Reptiles

And these are unclean to you among the swarming things that swarm upon the earth: the weasel, the mouse, the great lizard according to its kind, the gecko, the land crocodile, the lizard, the sand lizard, and the chameleon. (Leviticus 11: 29-30)

Rodents, reptiles, amphibians, insects and invertebrates are forbidden. The Bible does, however, cite four sorts of edible locust, difficult to identify today (Leviticus 11: 29-30). The bee is forbidden, but its honey is permitted.

Prohibition Against Eating Blood

The Torah forbids the consumption of blood: "For the life of the flesh is in the blood" (Leviticus 17: 11); "For the life of every creature is the blood of it; therefore I have said to the people of Israel, You shall not eat the blood of any creature" (Leviticus 17: 14). The medieval commentator Rashi (1040-1105) writes: "its blood is the principle of life, for life depends on it."

Blood is perceived as the material support of the animal soul, to be distinguished from the human soul. It would be sacrilege for man to consume blood because he must remain symbolically a superior being and not confound his soul with those of inferior beings. Jewish religious authorities have maintained for centuries that non-ritual slaughter (*shehita*) allows more efficient bloodletting. As we shall see later in this book, this view is rejected by modern science.

Prohibition Against Eating the Sciatic Nerve and Suet

The sciatic nerve of mammals is forbidden because of Jacob's wrestling with the angel: "Therefore to this day the Israelites do not eat the sinew of the hip which is upon the hollow of the thigh, because he touched the hollow of Jacob's thigh on the sinew of the hip" (Genesis 32: 32). The fatty parts from the rear of the animal are forbidden because they were burned on the sacrificial altar of the Temple in Jerusalem (Leviticus 4: 19). Since it is hard to remove the sciatic nerve and suet, kosher establishments only sell the fore parts of the animal.

11

Prohibition Against Mixing Meat and Milk

"You shall not boil a kid in its mother's milk"
(Exodus 23: 19 and 34: 26, and Deuteronomy 14: 21)

It is forbidden to mix meat with milk products. Milk, symbol of life (the food of newborns) and meat, for which it is necessary to kill, are antagonistic. So one must have two sets of kitchen equipment: one for meat products and the other for milk products. Crockery, of a different color if possible, is washed and stored separately. Fish can be cooked in milk and eaten in either sort of crockery. A third type of crockery called pareve (neutral) serves for foodstuffs that are neither meat nor milk based. After consuming milk products, one must wait a half hour to an hour to eat meat. The period is six hours after consuming certain hard or cooked cheeses. After consuming meat, one must wait six hours to consume milk products. For the sick and infants, these periods can be shortened.

Products of the land

All vegetable and cereal products are kosher except fruit from a tree during its first three years (Leviticus 19: 23) and one portion of bread or cake made with one of five cereals (wheat, barley, spelt, oats and rye), a portion once reserved for priests. The mistress of the house removes a small morsel of the bread or cake and burns it.[9]

Drinks

Fruit and vegetable juices are permitted. Cow's milk is authorized, but not donkey's milk. The Torah forbids consumption of drinks based on grapes or other pressed fruits which have not been produced under rabbinical control or which have been processed or handled by non-Jews. The same goes for vinegar, grapeseed oil or grape sugar. If a non-Jew touches certain ritually clean products, they become unclean and cannot be consumed.

Origin of Certification

Let us be clear that we are concerned here of the certification of kosher products and not of kashruth (the Jewish diet). Certification did not exist

12

when the Israelite people were formed, nor under David or Solomon, nor in the Kingdom of Judah, nor under Babylonian, Greek, Egyptian, Roman, Byzantine, Muslim, Ottoman domination, nor even under the British Mandate between 1921 and 1947.

Kosher certification appeared early in the 20th Century in the United States. And contrary to popular belief, the system of kosher certification was not invented by rabbis. We owe it to a true marketing genius.

Joseph Jacobs' Ingenious Idea

Kosher certification was invented in New York in 1919 by Joseph Jacobs. Born in April 1891, this New York Jew was the son of Aaron Fruyim Jacobs and Tillie Jacobs. He studied at City College and graduated in 1911. He began his career as a teacher at Morris High School in the Bronx. In 1916, at the age of 25, he tried to get promoted to the position of vice-principal. But he was not hired because he was considered too young.

Disillusioned, he left the teaching profession and became an advertising agent for the Jewish Daily Forward, a newspaper founded in 1897.[10] This New York daily was published in Yiddish under the name Forverts and in English under that of Forward.[11] Significantly for that historical period, this paper was a left-wing publication belonging to social democratic unionists and supporting the Jewish workers' movement. The paper's circulation reached 200,000 copies daily during the First World War. Jacobs was very successful as an advertising salesman and became the paper's Advertising Director. It was while looking for advertisers for the Jewish Daily Forward that he got the idea of offering his services to facilitate the sale of certain products to the Yiddish-speaking community of New York, at that time 1.5 million strong and unable to understand English.

In 1919, Jacobs founded the Joseph Jacobs Advertising Agency, Inc.[12], which still exists. It thus established itself as intermediary between producers of foodstuffs and Yiddish-speaking consumers. Jacobs translated the advertisements from English into Yiddish and was paid for helping the marketing departments of the big companies target their Yiddish-speaking customers. Moreover, the Jacobs Organization received commissions on space and time purchases in the Forward and other media.

To illustrate how Jacobs worked, let us take the example of coffee. At the time, religious Jews considered this vegetable matter, a bean, and thus not kosher for Passover. Jewish grocers classed coffee with *hamets* (forbidden for Passover) under the erroneous belief that coffee beans were *kitniyot*, when they are in fact the seeds of a fruit—and not beans. So Jacobs launched a publicity campaign to explain that coffee beans are not leguminous vegetables but fruits, and consequently kosher. He found a cooperative Rabbi to confirm his point of view and published announcements in the Yiddish papers. This is how Maxwell House became kosher[13]: without inspection or blessing.

On June 9, 1964 the journalist Sal Nuccio told the story of Joseph Jacobs in a business column in the New York Times:

> A close look at most food labels would reveal either a small "U" in a circle or an equally small "K," symbols that have wider currency in Metropolitan New York—and perhaps the United States—than the Lincoln penny. This may surprise almost anyone but the Jewish housewife, who looks for these symbols as assurance that the products she buys have been certified as kosher—or ritually clean—under rabbinical supervision. They appear on labels of billions of packages of food, beverages and soap sold each year. While both symbols indicate kosher certification, the "U" also means that the product has been certified by the Union of Orthodox Jewish Congregations of America. The man responsible for the wide currency of kosher symbols is 73-year-old Joseph Jacobs. He introduced a new dimension in grocery-product marketing and advertising when he founded the Joseph Jacobs Organization, Inc., 45 years ago this week. He described that dimension as the "complete promotion package for segment selling— specialized research and marketing plans to back up specialized merchandising and advertising techniques." His specialty was, and is, the Jewish market, which he believed could not be reached effectively without applying his then new "dimension."
>
> In 1919, Mr. Jacobs's market was made up of some 1.5 million Jews in New York, many of them Yiddish speaking immigrants who could be reached only through Yiddish language publications. These people, he said, had to be convinced of the kosher acceptability of big national and regional brands. To do this, the former high school teacher explained, "we suggested to manufacturers the use of rabbinical certification where necessary and possible, advertising appeals related to the Jewish way of life in Jewish media and special merchandising efforts in Jewish-area stores." The binding step was to imprint a kosher symbol on the label as it would appear and be explained in ads.
>
> Among the first companies to heed Mr. Jacobs's suggestions, it was said, were the Colgate-Palmolive Company, the Ralston Purina Company, Dugan's Bakery and the General Foods Corporation, for its Maxwell House

14

Coffee. Many others have since joined their ranks. Mr. Jacobs's company serves, in effect, as the Jewish-marketing department of manufacturers and their regular ad agencies. Itself structured like an ad agency, the company assists agencies in preparing programs and media schedules for Jewish markets. The agencies receive their regular commissions on space and time purchases, while the Jacobs Organization receives sales commissions from the magazines and other media used. Some 90 to 95 percent of today's Jewish media are in English, Richard A Jacobs, vice president of the company founded by his father, has found. Combined circulation of all Jewish publications, he said, has grown from less than a million in 1950 to about 2.2 million. Jewish listening to WEVD, he added, was "at its highest point since 1935, when his father placed the first sponsored program by a national brand on the New York radio station.

He noted that more than half of the nation's 5.5 million Jews live in Metropolitan New York. When asked whether the Jewish market as such may have been blended over the years with the total national market, the younger Mr. Jacobs said surveys have shown that the Jewish Market has retained its distinctive characteristics. "Perhaps it is because of a general religious resurgence," he said, "but whatever the reason, kosher-certified foods maintain their sales volumes and hotels and restaurants featuring kosher food are more prevalent than ever."

As for differences in preference, he added, "One study showed that the average Jews eats 21 pounds of cheese a year, compared with the national per capita consumption of 7 pounds. Further, our own study of 500 Jewish homes in this area showed that certain products that were traditionally shunned, such as lard and pork, still are not used." Joseph Jacobs began his career as a teacher at Morris High School in the Bronx after graduating from City College in 1911. Discouraged because his youth had eliminated him from consideration for promotion, despite his attainment of the highest grade among those taking an assistant principal's test, he became a space salesman on the Jewish Daily Forward in 1916. His marketing talents developed from there.[14]

Joseph Jacobs died March 26, 1967.

Kosher Meat "Gangstas" of Yesterday

We must go back a bit. Before becoming the industry it is today, the route toward the establishment of the kosher label was characterized at its beginnings by the violence surrounding the whole meat business. Perceived

15

as veritable manna from heaven, it led to ferocious, "anything goes" conflicts, even among Rabbis.

Controlling the Community in Montreal

In Montreal at the beginning of the 20th Century several Rabbis representing various interest groups fought to establish their leadership within the community. But a man has to live, and the Rabbis' only income was the salary they received for marriages, divorces, circumcisions, etc.[15] It did not amount to much. All had an interest in getting their hands on the revenue connected with *shehita*, i.e., kosher slaughter and certification.

In 1907, Rabbi Simon Glazer[16] accepted a position in Montreal and became director of the United Orthodox Congregations of Montreal[17], then head rabbi of the United Synagogues of Montreal and Quebec[18]. Consequently, he was the head rabbi of Montreal, Quebec and Canada and he was the first to attempt (in 1908) to regulate kosher certification in Montreal.[19] He was 30 at the time and known as a left-wing militant[20] who worked with labor unions.

Overseeing the Certification of Meat

Also in 1908, Rabbi Zvi Hirsch Cohen[21] (great-grandfather of the famous singer Leonard Cohen) founded the Montreal Kashruth Board[22] to challenge Rabbi Glazer's manner of regulating the certification of kosher meat. So two factions were competing to control certification. After ten years of struggle, a disgusted Glazer acknowledged defeat and left Canada for Seattle where he continued his career as a rabbi.

Another rabbi then entered the scene. Leah Rosenberg[23] (mother of the writer Mordechai Richler) relates that her father, Rabbi Yudel Rosenberg[24], a Toronto Talmudist and Kabbalist, took up residence in Montreal in 1919 mainly in order to decide the conflict within the kosher meat business, for even after Glazer left, the two factions were still opposed. But Rosenberg took sides with the faction opposed to Cohen and assumed the role of Glazer's successor. He created the kosher Council of Montreal[25], a body opposed to the Montreal Kosher Board[26], and recruited a number of *shochetim* (slaughterers) and butchers. He had 35 butchers supporting him, while Cohen only had 24.[27] Cohen continued the struggle and assumed leadership of the Montreal Council of Orthodox Rabbis[28], while Rosenberg was the head of the United Orthodox Congregations of Montreal[29].

In 1922 the two adversaries arranged a temporary truce in an effort to unite the community. They founded the Vaad Ha'ir, an umbrella organization including many religious and educational institutions in the Montreal Jewish community, at the time composed of about 60,000 inhabitants. The goal was to establish, in Montreal first of all, a *kehillah*, i.e., a parallel government for the Jewish community.[30]

But the battle quickly broke out once more. From 1922 until 1925, the rabbis, butchers and slaughterers faced off in what became known as the "Kosher Meat War."[31] Both leaders treated the other as traitors[32], meaning that they were unqualified to determine whether meat was kosher or not or to certify butchers—in short, they each maintained that the other's meat "was not kosher" and consequently denounced it as fraudulent.

Threats, Violence, Attempted Murder, etc.

First in the form of financial attacks, then verbal and written attacks, the Kosher Meat War degenerated and resulted in violence. *Shochetim* (certified slaughterers) who accepted the authority of the Vaad Ha'ir were threatened if they did not stop work. Dissidents recruited bully boys to convince the proprietors of various small-time butchers to close or remain open depending on their allegiance. Others were attacked in broad daylight. Rabbi Rosenberg was accosted by a furious mob who threw stones at him. A 1923 police report stated that one butcher, a supporter of Rabbi Rosenberg, struck a competitor in the head and left him for dead. He was caught and accusations of attempted murder were lodged against three representatives of the Association of Jewish Butchers. These methods were roughly those of organized crime. The Vaad Ha'ir slaughterers even received letters threatening to "shorten them by a head."[33] The Montreal newspaper Keneder Adler reported that the Association of Jewish Butchers had, with the approval of certain rabbis, employed gangsters to eliminate their rivals.[34] He was caught and accusations of attempted murder were lodged against three representatives of the Association of Jewish butchers. The methods were roughly those of organized crime

The mutual boycotting of rival factions of butchers and slaughterers became customary for several years. Each faction exhorted consumers not to purchase meat from its rivals. A typical example of this situation, a tract distributed in 1933, reported that a gang of butchers had attacked the innocent customers of a rival establishment. Several of the wounded required hospitalization. The tract stated: "Do not eat this meat. It is dripping with human blood!" But Cohen ended by winning the war and established a firm grip on the Jewish community and kosher certification. At Montreal, he would be the one to decide which slaughterers, butchers, slaughter-houses and butcher's shops would be certified kosher. Rosenberg became the vice president of the Vaad Ha'ir, an organization which still prevails in Montreal with its symbol MK.

Rumbles in New York as Well…

With its reputation as a violent town, it is not surprising that New York preceded Montreal in the establishment of a monopoly in kosher meat. Such a monopoly already existed in 1900. Abusing the gullibility of Yiddish-speaking immigrants, pious and respectful of tradition, those who controlled ritual slaughter became so powerful that there was no competition. The few companies belonging to the cartel fixed exorbitant prices to the detriment of the Jewish population of New York, who could not pay their prices.

Murmurs of Revolt

At the beginning of May 1902, the owners of about 1500 kosher butcher shops, members of the Hebrew Retail Butchers' Association, attempted in vain to boycott the wholesalers for two days to get them to lower their prices. The latter did not budge, and a great fight broke out, this time mobilizing tens of thousands of Jewish families. On May 15, 1902, women from the Lower East Side, no longer able to feed their children, along with their husbands, heroically descended into the streets and attacked butchers' shops, breaking windows and throwing meat into the street. They were protesting the most recent price increase from 12 to 18 cents a pound.

The "Great Kosher Meat Strike" had just begun.[35] Customers who failed to follow the rules of the boycott were attacked. Packets of meat were torn from their hands, thrown into the street and burned. Over 85 persons were arrested by the police, who tried to protect the shops and put an end to the mayhem. Three quarters of the persons arrested were women. After three weeks of a boycott disastrous for the wholesalers, the women succeeded in

18

getting the price of meat lowered by four cents, to 14 cents a pound. But despite this momentary retreat, the monopoly continued to operate.

In his book *On the Trails of Tradition: Explorations of Jewish Life and Learning*, the author Eliezer Segal, professor in the Department of Religious Studies at the University of Calgary[36], mentions that in 1927, just as the word racketeering was being introduced into the American legal vocabulary to describe the infiltration of business by gangsters, the list of industries involved included that of kosher meat, a market especially attractive to criminals.

And in fact, in 1929, 91 persons from the Official Orthodox Poultry Slaughterers of America and the Live Poultry Chamber of Commerce of New York, along with a dozen other individuals, were indicted under antitrust legislation for conspiracy to commit fraud.[37] The indictments specified the methods used to establish the monopoly: threats, violence against poultry sellers and their families, assaults, intimidation by means of bombs, inflammable matter and poison gas, armed robbery and spying in order to terrorize the entire poultry industry of Greater New York, a market active in more than twenty states with over $50 million worth of business in 1929.

Intimidation, harassment, violence, murder: these are the methods which the certifiers of kosher meat used at the beginning of the 20th Century in order to establish their authority and make themselves respected.

THE GREAT INVASION

A "Ghettoized" Dietary Tradition

For centuries, rabbis supervised only the production of kosher meat. Animals and poultry were slaughtered without prior stunning, as in Biblical times, by a *shohet* connected with a congregation or synagogue. Other foods, if they matched the criteria of kashruth, were eaten by the communities concerned. The insertion of kosher food in the world cannot be dissociated from Jewish migration. In 1654, New York, then known as New Amsterdam, received 23 Sephardic Jews. The Shearith Israel Synagogue supervised kosher slaughter beginning in 1752. In the middle of the 18th Century they were even exporting kosher beef to Jamaica and Curaçao![38]

19

A lieutenant in Gen. Amherst's army, Aaron Hart settled in New France after the British Conquest. He became a prosperous businessman at Trois-Rivières. In the course of fur trading expeditions with American Indians, he kept kosher food in his canoe.

From Age-Old Peddlers to Established Merchants

A second wave of Jewish immigrants arrived in the United States after 1830. Many practiced itinerant trading in the course of their travels across the continent involving non-perishable merchandise that was easy to transport such as spices, cloth, precious gems, and tableware—all things that could rapidly be carried off, a habit acquired by a people often faced with expulsions during its history. When they had enough money, some of these peddlers parked their carts and summoned their families to join them. The new Jewish communities created the institutions necessary to them and kept their own slaughterers. In Montreal, after 1880, Jewish immigration, until then mainly from Central and Western Europe, was overtaken by that from Eastern Europe. These Orthodox Jewish immigrants imported their own ancient religious practices. The first kosher slaughterhouse in Montreal opened in 1884.

In New York as elsewhere in America, Jews became active in the food industry; in particular, they opened shops. At the turn of the 20th Century, the range of kosher products on offer was no longer limited to meat and fish: it included bread, jam, soup, yeast, mustard, sauerkraut, soap, etc. In 1919, the Jewish advertising agent Joseph Jacobs sensed the financial potential and convinced entrepreneurs to put the "K" (for kosher) logo on their products. Another stroke of genius was Jacobs' subsequent integration of rabbis in the process of certification. The kosher industry was born.[39]

The Drift Toward Generalizing Kosher Certifications

In Montreal, New York, and elsewhere, Jews competed to seize control of the lucrative kosher meat industry. Rabbis saw in the certification of grocery products an opportunity to earn a salary the synagogues could not offer them. Thus, the logo "U" appeared on packages of food certified by the Union of Orthodox Jewish Congregations of America, along with those of other relevant certifying authorities: "O.K.", "Star-K", "COR", "MK", etc. More and more products that did not exist at the time of the Bible or

Talmud received the approval of rabbis: in 1923, Maxwell House coffee; in 1937, Coca-Cola. The same went for chocolate, ketchup, potato chips, Crisco shortening, maple syrup, dried cranberries, artificial sweeteners, Oreo cookies, etc.

In 1965, for the first time, makers of hot dogs and rye bread included non-Jewish consumers in their advertising campaigns. They claimed that the rabbinical seal signified "healthier, superior foods"—and thus, implicitly, better for you. These arguments have been hammered away at ever since. Within the space of a few decades, the rules of kashruth have become much more complex, to the point where one almost needs a chemical engineering degree to understand it. Today it amounts to an obsessive quest for antiseptic purity in which grocery products, threatened by microscopic toxic particles, must remain "chemically pure." Dry goods such as toilet paper, paper towels, aluminum foil, dishwashing soap, household soap, sponges, disposable diapers, etc., have come to be included in this maniacal expansion. The same goes for tank trucks, restaurants, cafés, catering services, hotels, etc. Some, including Conservative Jews, have been very critical of this seemingly never-ending spiral.[40] There are now even kosher suppositories[41], as well as dog and cat food[42]. In America, up to 50% of grocery products are kosher certified, for an estimated total annual sales of 500 billion dollars.

Apart from practicing Orthodox Jews, the majority of consumers pay no attention to the omnipresent kosher logos in their shopping carts.[43] But for how much longer will they unknowingly have to pay the costs of a business which is fueled, in the end, by paranoia disguised as religion?[44]

MK: The Certifier Vaad Ha'ir

Since 1967, the Jewish Community Council of Montreal[45], also known as the Vaad Ha'ir, has been responsible for the kosher certification "MK" of Beth Din of Montreal (a Jewish religious court) as well as the Ruth Institute (a program for converts). Directed by Rabbi Samuel Emanuel, the MK Agency certifies nearly 45,000 products and its 120 representatives are responsible for supervising 800 establishments. Products manufactured in Canada, the United States, Cuba, China, Italy and Azerbaijan are involved. Coca-Cola, Nestlé Canada, Unilever, Saputo, Parmalat, Smuckers and Kraft Canada are among the companies certified MK.

21

Kashruth or "Cash Route"—Myths and Realities

Companies are generally silent about the expenses they incur for certification and their impact on retail prices. Is there a confidentiality clause in the contract?

A sort of omertà exists regarding how much money certifiers earn from their activities, going as far as denying all profitability. For example, the CIJA (Centre for Israel and Jewish Affairs) attempts to dispel "mistaken beliefs" in this way:

> Myth: Revenue from the kosher food market finances the religious activities of the Jewish community. Reality: Revenues from the kosher food market profit the companies certified. The costs required by certification organizations only cover their inspection and other operations.[46]

Even the Bouchard-Taylor Report on Cultural and Religious Accommodation put in its two cents: "The additional costs assumed by consumers are quite minimal" and "rabbis make no profit from certification."[47] This dissimulation of the financial and communitarian aspect of the kosher certification business contradicts the very fundamentals of the Vaad Ha'ir of Montreal. Steven Lapidus, Associate Professor at the Canadian Institute of Jewish Studies at Concordia University and an authority on Orthodox Judaism produced a doctoral dissertation in 2011 that was very enlightening concerning the Jewish Community Council of Montreal (Vaad Ha'ir):

> On December 17, 1922, the Vaad Ha'ir of Montreal was officially founded to control Kashruth, Jewish education, labor arbitration, equity in Jewish business, and general governance of the community.... [T]he lack of sufficient remunerative positions for the city's rabbis led many to the most lucrative enterprise available to them at the time: kosher meat production and its supervision. Rabbinic competition, along with chaos in the kosher meat industry, were prominent impetuses in the founding of the Jewish Community Council and consequently, in its continued infighting. Besides using the income from kashruth supervision to defray the overhead costs of the Council, the founders of the Vaad would offer regular remuneration to the rabbis along with financial support for Jewish education in the city.[48]

Jacob Beller, author of *The Vaad Ha'ir—Montreal's Jewish Community Council—the Model of a Kehillah*, is cited by Lapidus on page 272: "Since its inception the Vaad Ha'ir has given generous aid to Jewish schools of all shades and to cultural institutions."

But this is not the most surprising thing. According to Lapidus, it remains a hotly contested point how representative the MK is even within the Jewish community, despite the ubiquity of its logo:

> Kashruth in Montreal, by the end of the millennium, had become a diverse and competitive field. Within the last several years, at least two Hasidic communities have developed their own kosher councils and their own identifying stamps – one from Belz and one from Satmar – appear on many food items prepared by the Hasidic community. The Tosher community of Boisbriand also supports its own separate kashruth council with the symbol TK standing for Tosh-kosher. Others symbols such as SK (for Satmar Kosher) or Belz (under the supervision of Rabbi Berel Volf Lerner of Machzikei HaDa'as) appear alongside the Vaad Ha'ir's MK, although the MK is not ubiquitously present on Hasidic foodstuffs prepared in Montreal, which is a clear indication that the Hasidic community is currently running competitive supervisory councils…. [I]ts status as the unique Kashruth authority in Montreal is now in question, as competing hashgachas [kosher oversight bodies] continue to increase. The Hasidic community in general tends to avoid relying on the MK and thus imports many items from New York with a better hekhsher [rabbinic testimonial], which will further erode the Vaad's singularity. It competes with Hasidic hekhsherim, both imported and local. Even meat which is not slaughtered under the MK but privately, or imported from outside Montreal, is reputedly available, albeit generally under the radar. (p. 258)

Lapidus specifies in a note on p. 258 "that a shohet had told him that he slaughtered calves for an American *hashgacha* also operating in Montreal. And that on April 1, 2010, the Canadian Jewish News reported that there were three or four kosher certification agencies in Montreal."

From Structure of Representative Power to "Local Sectarian Institution"

The Vaad Ha'ir, when founded in 1922, was an umbrella organization dedicated to the needs and interests of all members of the Jewish community. This structure, modeled on that of the Eastern European *kehillah*, was led by an equal number of representatives of all the groups involved, from progressive Jews to ultra-orthodox. In spite of these initial ambitions, the Vaad Ha'ir did not become the Jewish authority at a national level. In 1958, the Council greatly restricted its mandate: "To maintain and develop Orthodox Judaism and Jewish tradition in Greater Montreal and the Laurentians." Beginning in 1994, new rules for constituting the executive committee gave a larger part to Orthodox rabbis. Half its members became representatives of the Hassidic community.

The Vaad Ha'ir and, by extension, its MK kosher agency, thus became within a few decades extremely marginal institutions dominated by the most sectarian currents. This organization of questionable representativeness increased its intrusion into the Quebec food sector as never before. On its website, MK states: "The Vaad Ha'ir of Montreal offers a universally accepted kosher certification." Steven Lapidus's remarkable research suggests a quite different reality. MK is far from enjoying universal support, not merely within the Jewish community in general but especially among the 35,000 practitioners of kashruth. At what point does a commercial practice amount to false pretenses?

The Kashruth Council of Canada (COR):
The Sixty-Year-Old Elephant in the Grocery Store

The Kashruth Council of Canada (COR)[49] is the largest kosher certification agency in Canada. Its emblem, COR, stands for Council of Orthodox Rabbis. Active for the last sixty-five years, it supervises nearly a thousand establishments. Over 70,000 products bear the discreet symbol COR.[50] It is impossible to escape its overwhelming presence in all our grocery stores.

The administrative council of COR includes representatives of the Jewish community of Greater Toronto as well as the Vaad Hakashruth, a committee of Orthodox Toronto rabbis. They are the men who manage operations and fix the standards of kashruth.

Certification was organized in 1956 by the Council of Orthodox Rabbis, affiliated with the Canadian Jewish Congress (CJC), in order to control the lucrative and coveted kosher meat market in Toronto. During the 1940s and early 50s, anarchy prevailed in this sector. The CJC was asked to establish a system of supervision for kosher meat. In 1950, they created an orthodox division of ten synagogue directors called to sit on the executive committee presided over by Meyer Gasner. The committee instituted the Kashruth Committee with a mandate as follows:

1. To manage all forms of existing supervision by the Kashruth Committee; and
2. To put in place a program to raise awareness and tighten observance of the laws of kashruth.

In November 1952, the Kashruth Committee and the CJC approved the creation of a Kashruth Council of the CJC responsible for kosher certification. In November 1953, the Kashruth Committee asked the president to invite rabbis to participate in the Vaad Hakashruth. In 1954, the name Vaad Hakashruth of the Canadian Jewish Congress of the Central Region was adopted. Twelve rabbis sat on it. The rabbinic council of the Vaad Hakashruth has full authority on all matters concerning kashruth.

In June 1956, it assumed the name Council of Orthodox Rabbis affiliated with the Canadian Jewish Congress. The parties agreed to entrust administrative matters as well as custody of the kosher seals to the CJC and all religious questions relating to the application of Jewish Law (halakha) to the Vaad Hakashruth.

COR: A Powerful Lobby in Favor of Ritual Slaughter

At the beginning, COR undertook an intense campaign to lobby then-Prime Minister John G. Diefenbaker to get a law adopted to protect the technique of slaughtering animals without prior stunning known as *shehita*. Giving in to pressure from the local office of the Canadian Jewish Congress, the Diefenbaker government had the Bill of Rights adopted in 1960, the ancestor of our future charters of rights and freedoms.

In July 2000, the Orthodox Division of Federation (COR) registered itself as a non-profit legal entity and became the Kashruth Council of Canada.

Galen Weston's Pets

The Canadian supermarket chain Loblaws offers nearly 1500 kosher products among its in-house brand names President's Choice, No Name, and Blue Menu. Several of their stores in Ontario and Quebec have kosher departments that include bakeries, butchers' stalls and deli counters with full-time on site kosher inspectors. Some stores offer catering services and kosher cooking classes with the premises cleaned according to the laws of kashruth, distinct sets of cookware to avoid the mixing of meat and milk, and no activity on the Sabbath (Friday evening to Saturday evening).

In 2012, the board of Loblaws announced that all its kosher products would carry only the COR logo—instead of the dozens of logos previously found on their packages[51], and that it would only deal directly with the Kashruth Council of Canada, while allowing other supervisory agencies to continue to authenticating their respective products—thereby favoring the quasi-monopoly status of COR.

A LUCRATIVE RACKET?

A Colossal Fraud:
The Certification of Products Already Kosher

A billion dollars: such is the total price of kosher products sold in Canada [annually], a market which has risen 64% since 2003. This is not surprising, since 75-80% of grocery store items are certified. And since less than 1% of the population strictly observes kashruth, one may presume that the 99% of non-Jews for whom the products are not intended form a kind of "captive market."

From the time certification agencies took to certifying a multitude of products that did not need to be, sales have continued to rise explosively in North America, now a $15 billion annual industry. Under the heading Does it Really Need to be Kosher Certified?, Rabbi Tsvi Heber, Director of Community Kosher Operations for the Kashruth Council of Canada touches upon this delicate question:

> While kosher consumers surely reap the benefits of this expanded kosher market, it has also caused some confusion. Certifying intrinsically kosher products creates an impression that such products are not kosher unless they are certified. The reality is detergent obviously does not require kosher certification nor do many other foods, even some processed ones. Products like extra virgin olive oil, frozen blueberries, dried dates, unflavored beer and coffee, salt and pepper are kosher without certification. This knowledge is critical to travelers and to the rest of us when kosher certified products are not available or more expensive.[52]

However, one finds the COR logo on a good number of products "intrinsically kosher" whose certification is "useless."[53] For example, Sifto and Windsor salt, coffee brands such as Metro Irresistibles, Sunlight and Tide detergent, Metro Selection's Ultra dishwashing soap. In the corporate video Does Dish Soap Require Kosher Certification?, a representative of COR matter-of-factly states that dish washing soap does not require any certification. But this is only the tip of the iceberg: the list of unnecessarily certified products is a long one.

The Least Publicized List in the World

The Vaad HaKashruth of Denver, Colorado, publishes on its website a list of grocery items that need no certification, being "intrinsically kosher." The list includes, among other things: whole grain flour, sugar, spring water, herbs and spices, corn starch, oatmeal, fruits (fresh, frozen, or dried), whole grains, extra-virgin olive oil, pure fruit juice, cow's milk, vegetables (fresh or frozen), dried legumes, apple sauce, honey, eggs, baking powder, maple syrup, molasses, beer, tea, unflavored coffee, aluminum foil, paper towels, toilet paper and dish washing soap.[54]

But all these products are currently certified kosher! Take a look in your refrigerator or pantry and you will find plenty of them. Something is wrong here. Kosher logos even figure on dry goods. Shouldn't kashruth concern food exclusively? Is it sheer effrontery from the part of the rabbis or because the business community is utterly naive? And what part does sheer ignorance play?

"Part-Time Kosher" Toilet Paper

The Kashruth Commission, a division of the Chief Rabbinate of Quebec[55], seems to have occupied the toilet paper market niche! Its stamp KSR figures on the Cascades, Metro Selection and Sobeys Signal brands. But there is a sizeable problem: the toilet paper is not kosher during a 25-hour period each week due to the Sabbath! This is an obligatory weekly day of rest consecrated to God, from twilight on Friday until nightfall on Saturday. Tearing things is a violation of the Torah. By tearing any article, one is in some sense creating two of it.

Kosher Innovations, makers of Shabbos Bathroom Tissue, a pre-cut form of toilet paper, explains why it is forbidden to tear off toilet paper on the Sabbath:

> All things connected—whether by pressing, stitching or with a perforated line—must not be detached for use during the Sabbath. This would be to take something in one form and intentionally divide it into something else for certain purposes, thus creating something new. Tearing off toilet paper along a perforated edge creates a square of paper, violating the mechatech prohibition of the Torah. If one tears of a piece any old way (not following the perforation), this may be a violation of the *korei'ah* prohibition (tearing for constructive purposes).[56]

The pre-cut pieces of Shabbos Bathroom Tissue[57] can be used one-by-one. But nota bene: one must remove the cardboard oval from the top of the package before the Sabbath. And leaving conventional rolls of toilet paper may lead to accidental tearing by inattentive visitors, or those unaware of the Sabbath laws.

By the way, there even exists electric cookers certified kosher for the Sabbath.

Paper Towels: Finally Good to the Last Leaf!

Another part-time kosher paper product bearing the famous COR logo: SpongeTowels Ultra paper towels. An "enormous advance," if one is to believe Susan Sampson's article in the Toronto Star:

> Just in time for the big pre-Passover cleanup, SpongeTowels Ultra have been certified kosher. Many standard paper towels are glued to the tube with an adhesive containing starch that is not kosher for Passover for Ashkenazi Jews. They would have to avoid at least the last sheet, but now they don't have to worry about any contamination. No non-kosher animal by-products are used in the manufacturing of the paper towels, either. During Passover, corn, legumes and rice (known as kitniyot) are prohibited for Ashkenazi Jews (from Central and Eastern Europe). They are permissible for Sephardic Jews (Middle Eastern background). The Kashruth Council of Canada inspected the factory in Crabtree, Quebec, and certified the towels kosher. The maker, Kruger Products, says the change is a response to consumer demand.[58]

28

All this so that during Passover, the Ashkenazim no longer have to waste the last leaf of paper towel stuck to the cardboard roll with a corn-starch-based adhesive! Couldn't one conclude that it would be enough simply to leave the last leaf of each roll alone for the product to be kosher? What you don't know won't hurt you, runs the adage. According to Pierre Anctil, Professor of History at the University of Ottawa, "99% of consumers do not notice whether the products they buy are kosher, since the logos are not publicized."[59] The result is that the cost of universal kosherization or "kosher logomania" is necessarily borne by them. This situation is confirmed by the very rare references to the subject in the media. The journalist Michel Jean, of TVA, wrote in 2012: "As with the rest of kosher products, the bill is divided among the consumers as a group. Kevin Hart, owner of the bakery Homemade, estimates that this increases the cost of production by 5-7%. A bill which you, as a consumer, must of course pay."[60] In May 2014, Paul Lungen of The Canadian Jewish News (CJN), quoted an ex-employee of COR, Rabbi Moshe Bensalmon, a founding member of the certification agency Badatz: "He estimates that kosher food produced in Toronto "costs consumers 10 to 15 per cent higher [than it otherwise would be] because of COR."[61]

Bernie Bellan writes in the Jewish Post & News of Winnipeg: "We have become much more aware, for instance, of the tremendous competition that exists between the COR (Kashrut Council of Canada), which is Toronto based, and MK (Montreal Kosher). Both bodies are certifiers of kosher products and earn very substantial revenues as a result."[62] Nota bene: nearly 70 to 90% of the meat from ritually slaughtered animals ends up in the general [non-kosher] market without the slaughterer or certifier suffering financial loss. No notice of the method of slaughter figures on the package of those meats destined for non-Jewish customers.

An Investigative Journalist from the CJN Unmasks COR

In May 2014, Paul Lungen, a journalist with Canadian Jewish News, revealed the results of an eight-month investigation into the dubious commercial practices of the Kashruth Council of Canada (COR). CJN wanted to shed light on "the rumors, insinuations and allegations" circulating about COR.[63] It was a minefield: CJN was accused of committing the sin of *chillul HaShem* (profanation of the name of God). He [Lungen] defended himself in an editorial.[64] Owners of kosher establishments, food producers, suppliers and caterers described to the journalist their business relations with COR. Several complaints were mentioned: arbitrary rules which change without explanation, arbitrary pricing, false declarations concerning what is or is not kosher and unnecessarily costly demands. For once, we finally have precise figures on the financial aspects of kosher [certification]. We read that the Hubberts vegetable oil company suspended its contract with COR upon learning that its next bill would climb to $45,000. Between 2004 and 2008, Raphy Amar and Joelle Edery, owners of the kosher restaurant Gladstone's, closed their doors because operating expenses were too high, including payments of $2000 to COR. The hourly fee for supervising a caterer: $35-38; for institutional customers: $42-45. In 2003, COR had competition for supervising Sobey's grocery store in Thornhill. The Vaad Ha'ir of Montreal (MK)[65] offered to do the job for $100,000, i.e., about half of what COR was charging. The latter lowered their offer to $60,000 to retain the contract. In 2013, COR reported $5.4 million in revenues. Nine employees earned salaries of between $80,000 and $119,000, and one employee received between $120,000 and $159,000. Although COR is registered as a charitable organization, it allotted only $2500 to charity in 2013. The journalist also listed a number of incongruous details among the financial declarations of COR.

Rabbi Moshe Bensalmon, who was with COR for twenty years, founded the Badatz Toronto kosher certification agency in 2008 along with Rabi Amram Assayag from the Sephardic Kehila Centre. But COR warned the relevant companies and its own customers that if they signed with Badatz, their products would be rejected by all establishments where COR is present. Although its prices for supervision and certification are 10-30% less than those of COR, Badatz did not succeed in attracting many companies. Bensalmon is certain customers are paying too much at the grocery because of COR[66]. The Jewish Law dictates our conclusion in the Babylonian Talmud, under halakha (legal section), article 94a, it is written: "It is forbidden to lead people into error, even non-Jews."

Inspector-Rabbis: The New Knights of Cleanliness

Kashruth agencies cite the complexity of the procedures used by the modern food industry as a factor to justify their certification activities. The contemporary kosher diet is a vast extrapolation from ancient principles.

The foods permitted and the rituals involved have become an extremely complicated business, to the point of rendering "indispensable" the involvement of sterilization experts who hunt down microscopic particles: the inspector-rabbis. This drift into the maniacal and obsessive is strongly criticized from within the Jewish community itself, including conservative Jews: "You'll never get me to believe that minutiae which often borders on obsession and segregation is not a distortion of ethical objectives. Urging people to keep two kitchens at home in order to respect the separation of meat from milk is in my opinion a crazy distortion."[67]

Nevertheless, it is a source of income and well-paid jobs: an industry unto itself. [Note: *hashgacha* means surveillance; *mashgiach* means a kosher inspector.] We have seen a video[68] produced by the Kashruth Council of Canada (COR)[69] and recorded at Baycrest Hospital in Toronto, where one million kosher meals are produced each year with the strictest separation of meat from milk.

The *Mashgiachs* of the
Jewish Community Council of Montreal (MK)

The presence of *mashgiachs* in Canadian companies is not anything new, but in recent decades their number has increased tenfold due to the increasing ubiquity of the kosher label. Price scales depend on the level of surveillance necessary to maintain kosher installations, and varies between $4000 and $35,000 dollars per year. This certification must be renewed every year.[70]

The *mashgiachs* inspect ingredients and check that the equipment used does not touch non-kosher food. "Soy milk which passes through the same tubes as ordinary milk is contaminated, and thus no longer kosher," explains Rabbi Saul Emanuel. In this case, the company must agree to pour boiling water through all its tubes and not use them for at least 24 hours.[71] According to this site[72], eight food markets in Montreal have permanent on-site *mashgiachs*. The Montreal agency MK (Vaad Ha'ir) employs 120 overseers, and this number may increase because of the cuts the Harper government has made to the Canadian Food Inspection Agency (CFIA). These measures were accompanied by unprecedented financial support for a privatization of safety inspection services which will go to benefit rabbinical agencies such as MK.

The intrusion of clergymen into a domain well-served by the CFIA[73] and the MAPAQ[74], scientific regulatory bodies tasked with overseeing the quality of foodstuffs and empowered to declare recalls, thus enjoys the approval of Ottawa.

A Fine Conjuring Trick

Agriculture and Agri-Food Canada, through its Growing Forward policy, launched in 2009 a program of subsidies known as the *"Canadian Integrated Food Safety Initiative*[75]*,"* made to order for nonprofit organizations such as religious certification agencies. In November 2011, Minister Christian Paradis granted the Jewish Community Council of Montreal $763,650 to help it "develop improved safety processes for kosher foods".[76] And as if by magic... it became the Canadian Kosher Food Safety Initiative (CKFSI)[77]piloted by MK in partnership with the certification agencies Badatz Toronto, British Columbia Kosher, and Ottawa Vaad HaKashruth. According to the statement of the CKFSI, the project is "a national effort to harmonize kosher products with secular norms of food security."[78] From the webpage of CKFSI:

> At a time when Canadians are increasingly concerned about food safety, the goal of this initiative is to establish the kosher brand as a mark of quality and food safety. The Jewish Community Council, along with its partners across Canada, is working with manufacturers and food retailers to build on this solid foundation to the benefit of Canadians wherever they live and whatever their religious beliefs. In so doing, it is complementing the work of the Canadian Food Inspection Agency, which already applies the strictest standards to our food supply, and giving Canadians even more reason to have confidence in the safety and healthfulness of the food that reaches their tables.[79]

One of the specific elements of the CKFSI initiative is as follows: "The creation of the Digital Kosher Database, which will track ingredient lists, Kosher certificate updates, and certified kosher products to ensure they contain only kosher ingredients."[80] This is exactly what Canadian kosher certifiers have been doing for years; it is their modus operandi. Officially, the Kosher Initiative Project aims at sectors of food production little inspected by governmental authorities: "All kosher organizations participating have agreed to a set of norms relative to the inspection of bakeries, oil and confectionary products."[81] Is there another half-admitted goal? "The Canadian Kosher Food Safety Initiative will encourage the enlargement of the market for kosher foods beyond those consumers who depend on them for religious reasons. This market will thus reach all persons who want to ensure that the food they consume is safe—having been carefully inspected as to the quality of sources and production in compliance with the strictest standards."[82]

The statement by Canadian Jewish News confirms our worst suspicions: "Rabbi Emanuel said the initiative, which will complement the work of the Canadian Food Inspection Agency, is concerned with all types of foods, including meat, dairy, baked goods, beverages and produce."[83]

MK Pulls a Rabbit Out of its Hat, and voilà

The absence of the giant Kashruth Council of Canada (COR) among the agencies partnering with the CKFSI is far from innocent. The Jewish Community Council of Montreal (MK), which received nearly $4.2 million in subsidies between 2011 and 2019 from Agriculture and Agri-Food Canada, starts with praiseworthy intentions: "The first step of the initiative will be to create a Canadian Kosher council on food safety with a goal of standardizing food safety and traceability processes for the kosher industry. The different kosher marks will be invited to participate to ensure that no single kosher mark has a monopoly on certification."[84] But MK is positioning itself to do the opposite of what it announces.

In an interview granted to journalist Janice Arnold in November 2011, Rabbi Saul Emanuel "dreams aloud": "Asked if a long-term goal is the creation of a Canada-wide hechsher, Rabbi Emanuel replied that 'a national hechsher has been discussed. It certainly would be of great benefit,' but no concrete plans are in place at this point. [...] Rabbi Emanuel observed that the Vaad is well-positioned to take on this expanded, national role. Founded in 1922, the Vaad today has "the experience, capacity and technology to successfully implement this project." The MK has a new slogan: "Your key to a kosher Canada."[85]

Three years later, the Jewish Community Council of Montreal (MK) abandons its logo and trademark "MK Our Seal of Certification/Your Kashruth Guarantee." The seal it now puts on the kashruth certificates[86] it grants reads "MK Canada's Kosher Certifier/Certificateur casher du Canada[87]." MK thus proclaims itself "Canada's Kosher Certifier!" This is all the more curious from an organization whose representative character has shrunk like a cotton shirt in the wash since its creation in 1922, according to Prof. Steven Lapidus, authority on Orthodox Judaism who devoted his doctoral thesis to the history of the Vaad Ha'ir of Montreal.[88] The Jewish Community Council of Montreal (MK) is maneuvering to have its kosher certification (its safety norms and the involvement of its rabbi-inspectors) recognized by all retail establishments on the same basis as inspections by government agencies.

The rabbit MK is pulling out of its hat is called recognition, and the carrot: monopoly. The important thing is positioning oneself properly.

The Canadian Food Inspection Agency (CFIA) Gets "Sliced Up"

In 2016, the CFIA had its budget cut by 24% and its staff by 20%, equal to 1407 full-time positions. And the Food Safety Enhancement Program got 22% less in operating costs with 429 positions abolished, including inspectors, veterinarians, members of scientific and analytical teams, etc.[89] Nearly half the abolished positions were part of the CFIA based in Ottawa. Remarking on the loss of personnel in the national capital, Bob Kingston, president of the Agriculture Union of the Public Service Alliance of Canada, states that they would have a direct impact on the safety of food bought by Canadians:

For example, he cited the Ottawa-based unit responsible for approving meat product labels, which will be dismantled in favor of "downstream enforcement" involving inspectors catching fraudulent claims when products hit stores shelves. "After these cuts, Canadians can expect more fraudulent meat labels like we have seen for other products because CFIA pre-approval of meat product labels will be eliminated."[90]

Interventions After the Fact:
Small Comfort for Consumers

Economist David Macdonald of the Canadian Centre for Policy Alternatives, attacks both the cuts and the subsidies for the Kosher Initiative: "It is not the responsibility of a religious organization to determine the safety of the food you eat." He accuses Ottawa of using rabbis to privatize food inspection in the country. "We cannot have the same level of confidence," he believes. "If the government pays less for inspectors, we will have less well-trained, less experienced personnel."[91]

One man's meat is another man's poison! In a report by the television program J.E. broadcast in the Fall of 2012, it became clear that the Rabbinical Council of Montreal were rubbing their hands with glee. Rabbi David Bannon believes that the MK project will favor the development of kosher certification. "We will be able to certify the quality of the product for Jews and for the general population," he explains, adding that in his opinion it is an altogether "reasonable accommodation."[92] We also learn that the bill gets passed on to consumers, a fact corroborated by the owner of the bakery Homemade, who speaks of an additional 5-7% in production costs.

Recalls of Kosher Food: Yes, It Happens...

Kosher products are occasionally subject to recall for contamination by the Canadian Food Inspection Agency (CFIA). It goes to show the rabbis are not infallible. Kosher foods that "aren't kosher," then? Here are a few examples:

March 1, 2012: possible presence of Listeria monocytogenes bacteria in Glatt's brand of smoked beef BBQ sausages (certified MK)[93];

September 1, 2012: possible presence of E. coli 0157: H7 in certain Glatt's brand ground beef and veal products (certified MK)[94];

February 14, 2013: undeclared presence of mustard in certain meat products of the Continental Glatt Kosher brand (certified MK)[95];

May 30, 2014: recall of various products containing ground chia seeds contaminated by Salmonella Bacteria (certified U)[96];

June 18, 2014: recall of Al Fakher brand Tahini sauce sold by Sesameco at St-Laurent (Quebec) for Salmonella bacteria (certified MK)[97].

If Quebec Strawberries Could Talk...

MK seems to have a special grudge against Quebec strawberries. On July 13, 2011, it explained on its website how to wash our local strawberries before eating, at least until August 1 of that year. A maximum of 20 strawberries should be treated in one batch by cutting off the green top without making any hole in the center and soaking them four minutes in a liter of soapy water while rubbing them individually. Then rinse them in fresh water while rubbing each of them once again.[98] An alert published July 17, 2014 alleged that "highly infected" Quebec strawberries should not be eaten until further notice. But not a word about Floridian, Californian or Mexican strawberries, which often contain a high pesticide residue.[99]

Are Quebec's strawberries victims of discrimination? Are they really dirtier than their imported cousins? In any case, they are seeing red, and if they could move and speak, they would surely fight back amid their drastic bath, pleading in their own defense: "Your water isn't kosher, your water isn't kosher!..."

A Hard-line Approach Expressing a Refusal to Integrate?

In her February 22, 2013 article, Janice Arnold of the Canadian Jewish News reported the words of Rabbi Saul Emanuel:

> Rabbi Emanuel acknowledged that the mashgichim and CFIA inspectors are looking for different things, but there are areas of common concern, for example, verifying claims that products are lactose-free. The kashrut certifier has an interest in assuring that the product is pareve, that is, dairy-free, he said. He emphasized that mashgichim can complement the work of the CFIA, which had its budget cut by the government last year, but they cannot replace its inspection. "We cannot certify food safety," Rabbi Emanuel said. "But we are going to the same places anyway, we are asking some of the same questions, so maybe there can be a correlation." One result of this collaboration is that CFIA is now issuing public alerts that a company's products are not, say, pareve because traces of dairy were found in the assembly. The initiative was also about responding to the "tremendous demand" from the food industry for kosher certification. More and more producers of foods consumed by the general market, many from outside Ontario and Quebec, are applying, he said. He said these companies rightly view obtaining a kosher seal of approval as good business because the demand for kosher products has increased greatly in North America, mainly from non-Jews.[100]

"Are kosher food healthier than others?" Here is what the magazine *Protégez-vous* had to say in August 2002:

> In both cases, the quality is strictly the same, says France Provost of the Canadian Food Inspection Agency, for the rules of hygiene and health imposed by the federal government are the same for everybody. Solange

Doré of A. Lassonde, which produces Oasis orange juice confirms this: "The oranges used in our kosher juice are the same as in our non-kosher juice. The same goes for the cleaning of our equipment. The only difference is that in the one case, a rabbi handles the supervision, whereas in the other, it is done by one of our employees."[101]

The Kashruth Council of Canada has produced a 16-minute video *A Day in the Life of a COR Mashgiach* where we learn that "it is extremely dangerous to swallow a little insect." My dear rabbis, what would we do without you!

INSIDIOUS PROPAGANDA

Kosher for Whom?

According to Ira Robinson, professor of Religion at Concordia University, "kashruth is above all a symbol of communal solidarity. It allows Jews to be distinguished from non-Jews and creates a sense of belonging."[102] Does kashruth have little to do with nourishment as such? But business is thick-skinned. In Canada, kosher represents 70-80% of grocery products. Recurrent allegations and arguments inseparable from the rise of kosher certification in North America support the intrusion of that religious label into the public sphere. Whole production chains have been "kosherized."

A statistical glance at those declaring themselves Jewish by religion quickly tells us who is bearing the additional costs:

United States: of 270 million inhabitants, there are 1.6 million Jews, of whom 800,000 follow kashruth, i.e., less than 1% of the population.

Canada: of 35 million inhabitants, 329,000 are Jewish, i.e., less than 1% of the population. Of this small number, it is difficult to determine the percentage who observe kashruth (14-22% of 1%?);

Quebec: of 7.8 million inhabitants, 85,105 are Jewish, i.e., 1.1% of the population. They were 1.3% in 2001 and have continued to decline according to Statistics Canada.[103] The practitioners of kashruth, nearly 35,000 (i.e., 0.5% of the total population), do not form a unity.

The main interested party, the certification agency MK[104], acknowledges through the voice of Rabbi Saul Emanuel that it does not know the exact number of people following kashruth: "The Vaad estimates that 20 to 25 per cent of Montreal Jews are strictly kosher, both in their home and outside, but is really not certain about that," Rabbi Emanuel said. "I wish someone would do a study."[105] "What percentage of the Montreal Jewish community keeps kosher?," he is asked. While the rabbi said he could not give precise figures, noting he would love to see a formal study done on the topic, he estimated that as much as 25 percent are kosher in the strictest sense.[106]

Rabbi Saul Emanuel's admission of ignorance is consistent with the bulletin of the Canadian Kosher Food Safety Initiative of June 2012: "In fact, statistics show the majority of kosher food is not bought and consumed by Jews."[107]

A Real Advertising Bonanza

So one must cite something besides the Jewish lobby's reputation for pugnacity in order to understand the generalization of the kosher label. The key is found in advertising and the evolution of modern marketing. During the first half of the century, the promotion of kosher products was aimed only at observers of kashruth. Seeking to seduce Jewish housewives, ads vaunted the supposedly "superior attributes" of kosher. But a bold advertising gambit would bring it definitively into all grocery baskets.

In 1965, the Hebrew National hot dog company carried out a vast advertising campaign in which the attributes of kosher products were used to differentiate them from non-certified products.[108] Their slogan *"We answer to a higher authority"* suggested reasons why kosher products might be equally attractive to non-Jewish consumers: the intervention of an agency which, above and beyond governmental inspection, makes doubly sure of the healthiness of kosher foods, especially meats. Hebrew National was the first company to dare to present kosher as intended for all customers without exception.

Levy's rye bread followed in its wake with a similar advertising campaign. Their slogan *"You don't have to be Jewish to like Levy's"* was printed in giant letters on its advertisements, some of them depicting an American Indian chief eating bread. Levy's also claimed that the rabbinical seal signified "superior, more healthful ingredients."

The association of the kosher seal with high quality for all consumers, born of an advertising campaign, is still exploited in the discourse of certifiers and their partners.

Certifiers Lay It on Thick

The kosher certification agencies fuel similar myths, echoing one another, tossing the same eternal salad to justify a parasitic system which has become a lucrative business for them. The arguments they use to get this predation and intrusion accepted in the public commercial realm, although prejudicial to the secularism of the state, are of a disarming presumptuousness. Here are a few samples:

> Whoever wants to eat good food buys kosher (Avrom Pollak).[109]

> Eating kosher means rising to the challenge of having a healthy mind in a healthy body (Bruno Fiszon, Chief Rabbi of Metz and the Moselle).[110]

> If eating is a right for the Torah, it is also a duty, for one must be in good health to serve and carry out the divine will. Thus, regarding food, eating and drinking for one's own satisfaction, even of permitted goods, is not praiseworthy. This is why one does not eat everything one's palate might desire, as animals do, but profitable things good for the body" (Grand Rabbinate of Quebec, Kashruth Commission).[111]

But we shall leave to the Jewish religious authorities the job of evaluating the degree of divine approbation gained by the consumption of such quintessentially kosher foods as Coca-Cola, Frito's corn chips, Krispy Kreme doughnuts, Cadbury's chocolates, and Kraft Macaroni & Cheese. Does "kosher" also rhyme with "junk food?" Or have we pagans failed to understand something?

Highly Sought Out Yet "Invisible" Certifications

The most insidious claim circulating amid the flood of pro-kosher propaganda relates to the supposedly increasing attraction the logo has for consumers. "While there are certainly many more kosher consumers today than in years past, the surge in variety of kosher products has more to do with the power of 'kosher,'" says Rabbi Tsvi Heber on the COR website.[112] "Although kosher food is not yet considered mainstream, steady increases in consumer demand ensure opportunities for further expansion in both the domestic and export markets," we read in MK's advertising supplement in

39

Canadian Grocer, October 2012. "Growth in this market is exponential," adds Rabbi Saul Emanuel.[113]

Moreover, the bulletin of the Canadian Kosher Food Safety Initiative (CKFSI) of January 2012 explains this program subsidized by Ottawa as follows: "The project is based on the fact that Canadians have already shown confidence in kosher certification as an indicator of quality and food safety."[114] Two studies of kosher food in the United States are cited in the same bulletin, one by Agriculture and Agri-Food Canada (August 2010) and another by Mintel, a market study firm with offices in London and Chicago. According to the former, 55% of American consumers believe kosher products are safer and better for one's health. The statistics cited by the second group are just as euphoric: 62% of consumers buy kosher food because of its quality, 51% for reasons of health, and 34% because they are safer. This data is repeated in the supplement to Canadian Grocer cited above.

MK refrains from citing the striking Chaire Bombardier report from Sherbrooke University which ranks agrifood quality labels. And for good reason! We learn there that religious labels "pass almost unnoticed by the general population."[115] Yet Rabbi Saul Emmanuel continues to assert in the media that increasing number of consumers "seek out" kosher products.

MK: The Frog That Wanted to Be as Big as an Ox

MK, managed by the Jewish Community Council of Montreal (Vaad Ha'ir), has big ambitions. A close examination of this kosher agency is necessary, given the breadth of its aims and the political support it enjoys. In spite of the similarities between the ways they promote themselves, MK and the Toronto giant COR (Kashruth Council of Canada) are perpetually at war. As in La Fontaine's fable of the frog that wanted to be as big as an ox, MK will stop at nothing to outcompete its rival even on its own turf, as seen in 2009 when COR lost its supervisory contract with Air Canada and Pearson Airport, who preferred MK, who were already present in some twenty Ontario businesses.[116] An investigative journalist revealed some interesting details concerning this switch: specifically, the names of Elaine Rovinescu, wife of Air Canada's CEO, and of liberal Senator Celine Hervieux-Payette, both shareholders of the Medina, Inc. quality assurance system, consulting partners of MK. The corporation voluntarily dissolved itself March 30, 2012. According to the Quebec Business Register, it was an internet-based food auditing firm. It was also one of the private suppliers of the Canadian Kosher Food Safety Initiative (CKFSI).[117]

MK, never at a loss, is generating its own myth of nationwide authority and seems to have ended by believing it, in view of the logo change it has carried out on kosher certificates it now issues to the businesses it certifies, proclaiming itself "Canada's Kosher Certifier." The verdict of the above-mentioned Steven Lapidus is without appeal. Founded in 1922 to operate for the sake of all members of the Jewish community, the Vaad has become a purely Hassidic institution, disregarding the diversity among its fellow Jews. It applies the Jewish Law systematically and in a draconian fashion. "Sectarian and conformist," such is the Vaad today, dedicated to preserving its Hassidic identity by means of an infrastructure centered on kosher certification. Worse, MK has recently taken to offering another type of kosher certification under the label MK Mehadrin, supposed to be even stricter than the mere MK certification. The Vaad decided to create an even superior level of control.[118]

So there are now two categories of kosher products! Must we conclude that the previous one, with the simple MK logo, was not really kosher? At a time when the Hassidic community can buy plenty of products certified by competing rabbinical authorities, how can MK advertise itself as "Canada's Kosher Certifier?"

Money Questions and Accusations of Anti-Semitism on Autopilot

The arguments used by certain interest groups to deny the existence of a kosher religious tax, notably by resorting to the term anti-Semitism, are inspired by an Anti-Defamation League (ADL) text, The Kosher Tax: Anti-Semitic Recipe for Hate (1991). This tax is there said to be nothing by a "hoax:"

> The bizarre claim by right wing extremists that kosher certification markings on food product labels ("U", "K," etc.) cost consumers extra money and represent, in effect, a 'kosher tax' to make rabbis rich, is a striking example of the propaganda used by anti-Semites to trick the uninformed into accepting conspiracy charges and stereotypes about Jews. Other anti-Semitic allegations regarding kosher designation on foods include charges that 'the kosher food racket' benefits Jewish organizations while only a small segment of the American population desires such markings....[119]

41

Here are the villains with whom all critics of kosher certification are henceforth associated:

> The most active right-wing extremist sources of the "kosher tax" hoax are various Ku Klux Klan groups and the National States Rights Party, based in Marietta, GA. The Invisible Empire Knights of the Ku Klux Klan (now based in North Carolina), through its Empire Publishing, offers a pamphlet titled "The Kosher Food Swindle" to its members and supporters.[120]

The horror! In 1990, Edward Fields, a "notorious ultra-nationalist activist," dared to write this about kosher certification: "All of this is superstitious nonsense and has absolutely nothing to do with improving the quality of any food product. Still, this clever scheme of requiring kosher labeling has become a multi-million-dollar business today!"[121] Despite the pertinence of this remark, Fields is condemned to be wrong always, since a priori an "extremist" can never say anything sensible. This, at any rate, is how the extremely biased ADL reasons, rather than responding honestly to the points raised. According to these rules, no one will be justified in its eyes, but only earn the instant label anti-Semite, a serious accusation which, in reality, is only justified in a few particular, isolated cases.

Founded October 20, 1913 in the United States, the Anti-Defamation League is a controversial extension of B'nai B'rith. A book published in 1992 by Executive Intelligence Review[122], *The Ugly Truth About the Anti-Defamation League*, exposes the murky foundations of the ADL[123]. Although it is outside the scope of the present work to confirm or reject the thesis of this book, the scope of its supporting evidence corroborates the saying that where there is smoke, there is fire.[124] The all-purpose explanations of the defenders of kosher certification rely upon the supposed rigor and objectivity of the ADL article—even if they do not cite it directly—whose credibility is practically nil. The aim is to inculcate in consumers' minds that the costs of kosher certification are infinitesimal. The ADL's central argument to the effect that the kosher tax is a "hoax" is the following:

> The cost to the consumer for this service is a miniscule fraction of the total production overhead; it is so negligible in practical terms as to be virtually non-existent. A May 18, 1975 New York Times article reported that the cost to General Foods' "Bird's Eye" Unit, for example, is

6.5 millionths (.0000065) of a cent per item. Furthermore, a representative of the Heinz Company has said that the per item cost is "so small we can't even calculate it," and that such labeling actually makes products less costly by increasing the market for them.[125]

But if the expense of certification is this low, why has no business ever revealed the exact figures? And why don't the Jewish communities which demand certification pay the costs themselves? The ADL cites General Foods' Birds Eye frozen products. The Lilliputian percentage of .0000065 cents for unit is chimerical. A certifier would run to General Foods to collect $6.50 on every million sold, not enough to keep one's gas tank full! But if "per item" means not each package but each pea, grain of corn, piece of carrot or broccoli florets it contains, we would get credible figures.

It is impossible to take the ADL's allegations seriously in view of an article which appeared March 20, 2003 in the Canadian Jewish News, *"Heinz Canada Trims Kosher Product Line:"*

> Kosher shoppers were shocked recently to discover that Heinz Canada has removed kosher certification from all but a handful of its products. According to company spokesperson Anna Relyea, the move stemmed from a desire to "keep costs down while continuing to provide kosher products to our customers. This was done after a lot of careful consideration," she said. "Only when there were no other options available did we decide to remove the designations." Items that are no longer kosher include staples such as tomato sauces and paste, vinegar and mustard. Heinz jarred baby foods are also no longer kosher, and Heinz – as the federal Competition Bureau noted three years ago when it investigated the company for anti-competitive practices in the sector – is the sole supplier of jarred baby food in Canada. Heinz Canada has also discontinued supervision on all domestic beans, including those formerly manufactured under the Libby's label. Products were cut from the kosher line based on a variety of factors, Relyea said, including "how complex the manufacturing is, what the savings were and so on." Relyea called the Canadian marketplace a "very competitive retail trade environment," one that keeps the company "under continual pressure to keep costs down to remain competitive."[126]

The mere fact that there is fierce competition between the 273 kosher certification agencies in the United States[127] and between dozens of others in Canada stands as a witness to the amounts of revenue at stake.

In 2013 the Kashruth Council of Canada (COR) declared revenues of $5.4 million, and nine of its employees earned salaries of between $80,000 and $119,000, while one employee made between $120,000 and $159,999.[128]

A Quebec Philosopher Goes Through the Wringer!

To know who rules you, it is enough to look at those you cannot criticize.

– Voltaire

Gather thistles, expect prickles! Anyone who dares to utter the least criticism of kosher certification calls down upon himself the usual anathemas of racist or anti-Semite. Broadcast by the media in March 2014, calumnies rained down on philosophy professor Louise Mailloux, at that time a candidate of the Parti Québécois for the Montreal electoral district of Gouin in the Quebec general election of April 7. In the course of a talk show, she had spoken of a "religious tax" and the use presumably made of the money without consumers' knowledge.[129] The ferocity of the response by certain Jewish interest groups demonstrates that she had hit the target. The Quebec branch of the Centre for Israel and Jewish Affairs (CIJA) echoed the ADL whose arguments in defense of certification it reproduced literally:

> In a Thursday statement, the Quebec branch of the Centre for Israel and Jewish Affairs accused Ms. Mailloux of echoing "a conspiracy created and spread by the Ku Klux Klan, and championed by many other racist and neo-Nazi groups." Although theories vary, the premise of the so-called kosher tax is that Jews extort food companies for the cost of certification, and then pass on the funding to Zionist causes. As a KKK pamphlet cited by the Anti-Defamation League writes "Jews have discovered a way to coerce business to pay taxes directly to Jewish organizations and pass the cost on to the consumer." In reality, while kosher and halal certification is not free; food companies do it for the same reason they would claim a product is low fat or GMO-free: to open up a new market segment and boost sales.[130]

Two weeks later, the ADL called Ms. Mailloux and the political class of Quebec anti-Semites in a press release:

The notion of a "kosher tax" is a decades-old extremist conspiracy theory claiming that kosher certification on food product labels forces consumers to pay extra for the financial benefit of religious individuals and institutions. In actuality, the cost to the consumer for this service is a miniscule fraction of the total overhead production.[131]

Old arguments that were recycled once again by Rabbi Zvi Hershcovich of the website Bill 613 [www.bill613.com] to smear journalist Pierre Lacerte who had dared to add detail to Ms. Mailloux' remarks[132]:

During the recent election in Quebec, PQ candidate Louise Mailloux earned international condemnation from politicians, media outlets, and tolerance organizations for bringing up a myth created by Ku Klux Klan and Neo-Nazi groups alleging that citizens were unwittingly paying a "Kosher tax" on foods certified by a Rabbinic authority. Ultimately, Mailloux was defeated, and supporting her racist comments may be one reason the PQ lost so drastically in the election. The Kosher Tax myth has been disproven many times. Not only is the cost of certification minimal, it doesn't affect the pricing since companies that pay for the certification see their sales rise being that their product will now be purchased by religious Jews and Muslims, as well as (in many cases) vegetarians and others with health concerns. Acquiring kosher certification is a wise business decision, a way to get ahead of the competition and reach a wider audience. It's business, plain and simple. If it weren't so, then consumers would purchase the products without certification and put the certified company out of business.[133]

Now, Louise Mailloux had never preached any sort of theory from the Ku Klux Klan. This was an extrapolation and distortion of what the philosophy professor had actually said, and therefore a gratuitous libel of her. What they were really aiming at was proposed Law 60 which sought to institute norms for religious accommodation and a legal basis for the secularity of Quebec Province. Those who had really spread material from the Ku Klux Klan never made the front page of Quebec newspapers during the electoral campaign of 2014. According to the National Post, in 2011, the Shiite group Canadian Shia Muslims Organization (CASMO) had posted on their site a video by David Duke, former Ku Klux Klan Leader.[134] But one member of CASMO attacked Ms. Mailloux during the campaign.[135]

45

The Pinocchio Quiz

"Follow the money," as the saying goes. The thorny question of how the sums collected by kosher agencies are used remains a taboo subject. Non-Jewish consumers, the principle purchasers of kosher products, are kept in ignorance. And this explanation by the Centre for Israel and Jewish Affairs (CIJA) is hardly going to dissipate the confusion:

> "Myth: Revenue from the kosher food market finances the religious activities of the Jewish community. Reality: Revenue from the kosher food trade benefit the companies certified. The fees charged by the certification agencies are only used to carry out their inspections and business operations."[136]

But this statement by the CIJA is contradicted by a European Jewish website: "These certifiers are very numerous and try through advertising and commercial activities to make their own logo the best known. These are a few of the certifications of the principle communities of Paris, Canada, the US, but in every country there are plenty of them, for it is a market and the profits support the institutions of each group or association."[137] The ADL's press release of March 2014 takes offense at the statements by philosopher Louise Mailloux: "Louise Mailloux, a philosophy professor and PQ candidate in the upcoming April 7 provincial elections, told reporters that she stood by prior statements promoting the canard that there is a so-called "kosher tax," for the financial benefit of the Jewish community. Ms. Mailloux referred to kosher and halal certification as "theft" and a "religious tax" directly paid to religious institutions."[138]

Rather than gratuitously attacking Louise Mailloux, the ADL and CIJA ought to have taken notice of the work of Steven Lapidus, Associate Professor at the Institute for Canadian Jewish Studies at Concordia University and an authority on Orthodox Judaism. The concealment of the financial and communitarian aspect of the kosher certification business contradicts the fundamental principles of the Jewish Community Council of Montreal:

On December 17, 1922, the Vaad Ha'ir of Montreal was officially founded to control Kashrut, Jewish education, labor arbitration, equity in Jewish business, and general governance of the community. [...] Besides using the income from kashrut supervision to defray the overhead costs of the Council, the founders of the Vaad would offer regular remuneration to the rabbis along with financial support for Jewish education in the city.[139]

According to researcher Jacob Beller, "Since its inception the Vaad Ha'ir has given generous aid to Jewish schools of all shades and to cultural institutions."[140] Already in 2006, Catherine Handfield had written this in the newspaper Montréal Campus:

> After paying its inspectors, the five major kosher certification agencies of North America donate a part of their profits to Jewish charity organization. The Jewish Community Council of Montreal has its own foundation which aids the poorest practitioners of Judaism in Montreal and in Israel. These charitable organization also have an educational wing. "We help maintain Jewish education both here and in Israel," says Rabbi Saul Emanuel.[141]

So the Jewish Community Council of Montreal has a foundation!

Finally, we must look at this organization which stated in March 2014 that Louise Mailloux was spreading an anti-Semitic theory of the Ku Klux Klan. The Centre for Israel and Jewish Affairs works in partnership with the Federation CJA, the largest Jewish communitarian philanthropic organization in Canada ($48.8 million in receipts for 2014, of which $6 million was allotted to Israel[142]). To cite just one interesting ramification, Rabbi Reuben Joshua Poupko, administrator at both CIJA and CJA[143], is involved with the Montreal branch of the Jewish National Fund, a Zionist foundation dedicated to purchasing land to enlarge the State of Israel[144].

CIJA Keeps Its Eye on the Ball

On its web page "Myths and Realities of Kosher Certification," CIJA follows the ADL playbook:

> ...Others repeat the myth concocted by neo-Nazi groups that kosher certification is a religious tax exacted by Jews without their fellow-citizen's knowledge. Myth: Kosher certification agencies persuade companies to get certified. Reality: it is companies who solicit kosher certification to open new markets for their products. Myth: Kosher certification is a form of religious tax, because it raises retail prices. Reality: Kosher certification is a marketing strategy of the certified companies. The costs of certification are minimal when measured against

47

the general costs of production and do not inflate retail prices. In fact, kosher certification opens up new markets and brings in revenue for certified companies, which contributes to lowering retail prices. Moreover, kosher certification is valued by vegetarians and vegans, who recognize in it a guarantee that products certified as neither meat nor milk do not contain any animal matter.[145]

Now, anyone who employs financial arguments leaves himself open to a response that gets down to brass tacks. Just what market are we speaking about? The certification business rests entirely on the myth of a constantly expanding kosher market. The exact number of kosher practitioners in Quebec is unknown, by the admission of Rabbi Saul Emanuel, spokesman for the MK agency, who estimates it at 25% of the Jewish community even as he regrets the lack of studies on the subject.[146] The only certainty is that the Jewish population is declining in Quebec, according to the data of Canada Statistics. Between 2001 and 2011, it went from 89,915 to 85,105.[147] Now, according to the Léger poll on religion presented on the television program TVA Nouvelles on April 22, 2015, 90% of Jews in Quebec describe themselves as non-practicing. How many Jews buy exclusively kosher? 10,000? 20,000? 30,000? And since there are various levels of kashruth, Bishul Yisroel being the strictest, and different certifiers according to the preferences of different communities, we may ask just what clientele is targeted by the MK and COR labels omnipresent on grocers' shelves. Could it be just a phantom market?

To hear Rabbi Saul Emanuel tell it, companies "are increasingly numerous" in wanting certification. This is supposedly tied to the "considerable" growth in consumer demand, especially non-Jewish, for kosher products[148]: "the attraction of kosher for today's consumer is much broader, extending, e.g., to vegetarians and persons suffering from allergies or lactose intolerance."[149]

Is Quebec unusual in this respect? According to a 2012 joint study carried out by Canadian and French institutional research teams, religious labels are hardly noticed by the general population. The three labels most sought after by the public of Quebec are, in order, Aliments Québec, Pommes Qualité Québec, and Aliments préparés au Québec.[150] The other customer groups alleged by kosher certifiers represent a very tiny percentage of the population and to our knowledge there is no study indicating that vegetarians/vegans, persons suffering from lactose intolerance/food allergies, or Muslims look expressly for kosher labels. The identification of allergenic or potentially toxic ingredients is in any case systematically regulated by either the Canadian Food Inspection Agency or Quebec's Ministry of Agriculture, Fisheries and Food. So is food safety. Kosher inspection changes nothing.

An Implicit Obligation for Our Businessmen

There is good reason to think many businessmen would gladly do without these costly and laborious procedures. But the big supermarket chains are authoritative and dictate the rules for getting onto their shelves. Without explicitly saying it, it is clear they encourage kosher certification. This has been confirmed for us by businessmen who say they have been pressured into getting certified. Grocery chains such as Loblaws demand that all their suppliers be certified. This demand forces smaller businesses to spend thousands of dollars to obtain a certification which affects less than 1% of the population. The food business is implacable: any deceptive product will be withdrawn from shelves, kosher or not.

Only large firms, it seems, can afford certification. How far can they avoid passing costs on to consumers remains to be seen. We have often heard that these amounts figure in the marketing budget and expenses column:

As for the charge that has repeatedly appeared in the French-language media that kashrut is increasing food costs for everyone, Rabbi Emanuel counters that what companies pay to the Vaad is spread over such volume as to be infinitesimal per unit, if that. In fact, he believes no actual cost is passed on to the consumer because companies absorb it in their marketing budget.[151]

Very different are the words of Rabbi Moshe Bensalmon of the Badatz certification agency, who estimates that kosher foods produced in Toronto coast 10-15% more than they should because of COR's high certification fees.[152] In 2011, the Dare company began by turning down a request from Jewish mothers in their daughters' names for kosher cookies to be sold as part of a fundraising drive by the Girl Guides of Thornhill. An extract from the letter from Girl Guides Cookies: "Although the ingredients are kosher, Dare equipment is not. The kosher certification is very expensive, over and above the annual cost required to maintain it. We are refraining from certifying these products because the costs greatly outweigh the benefits. We are sorry, but making these cookies kosher is not a good business decision."[153] Dare later went back on this decision and now has its premises certified. It would be interesting to know why.

The case of Raphy Amar and Joelle Edery, proprietors of Beverly Hills Catering, is compelling. Between 2004 and 2008 they had a kosher restaurant called Gladstone's which went bankrupt due to excessive operating costs, including monthly payments of $2000 to COR.[154]

The Market for Kosher Products: Open in Only One Direction?

According to one of our sources who prefers to remain anonymous, the certification process is much more onerous for small businesses. The newspaper Les Affaires reported in 2011 that the dessert company Aliments Ange-Gardien, founded by Julie Larochelle, had acquired MK certification in order to reach the New York market:

> Aliments Ange-Gardien obtained kosher certification last year following an approximately 12-month process that included revising its ingredients and manufacturing procedures. Since then, a Rabbi visits the factory each month for the customary verification and blessing. So far, these procedures "have not had any major impact on sales," the owner admits. However, Julie Larochelle is convinced that this medium or long-term investment—for which she declines to cite figures—will end up paying off. "It's not that complicated and it allows us to develop markets."[155]

But the MK-pareve logo was no open sesame! Driven to bankruptcy, the company was bought out in January 2013 by Hypo Délice and Je Reçois Traiteur... A revealing fact: they did not renew their kosher certification, resting satisfied with international HACCP food safety norms.

> One may remember that the announcement of Aliments Ange-Gardien's closing in December 2012 sent shock waves through Quebec's allergy community (there was even a petition in Boucherville to try to save the company). Julie Rochelle, who founded Aliments Ange-Gardien five years ago, explained that economic reasons and several missed appointments were the basis for the closing.[156]

Not only did the MK label fail to open any markets for them, but one of their former suppliers confirmed for us under cover of anonymity that this kosher certification burdened Larochelle's business and she had to suffer financial losses in the adventure. Our witness also reports that the monopolistic practices underlying the kosher tax system definitely disfavor small businesses, which are relegated to local markets. The most ironic (or shocking?) thing is that the majority of merchandise sold in Jewish groceries is of foreign manufacture, especially American.[157]

Among the most famous we may cite Lipa's Supermarket on Park Avenue in Montreal which serves the Hassidic community of Outremont. The MK and COR logos are rarely found in this store. Quebec's kosher market seems to flourish to the benefit of its southern neighbors.

Fast Food Restaurants Swimming Against the Current

Spokesmen for the big supermarket chains often cite profitability to justify the presence of kosher certifications. If they are essential for maximizing profits, why don't fast food restaurants, whose sole aim is profitability, follow in their footsteps? If kosher certification is so profitable, why don't Burger King, Subway, McDonald's, Tim Horton's and others operating in Quebec offer kosher menus? Only Second Cup, an establishment in Montreal's Jewish General Hospital, is certified kosher.[158]

Organic Wild Blueberries: A Double Standard?

The Quebec company Bleuets Mistassini Ltée[159] produces more than 13,600 tons of frozen wild blueberries annually. They are the fourth largest producer of frozen wild blueberries in the world, exporting to over 30 countries. Their organic blueberries are certified kosher, but not those of their competitor! Health Valley frozen wild blueberries, a brand belonging to Hain Celestial Group, Inc., a publicly traded company based in New York State, are widely available in Quebec. The absence of the kosher label does not prevent Health Valley from exporting. So why must Quebec blueberries prove their acceptability to the world?

The Great Bluff: Taking the Part for the Whole

Certification was imposed by restricting kashruth to the domain of food, but the Torah also forbids wearing a garment of mixed wool and linen. This is called *chaatnez*. A rabbinical prohibition also applies to rugs, napkins, and tablecloths. This rule is part of houkim (rules non amenable to human reason). In larger Jewish communities there exist *chaatnez* laboratories in which overseers take a piece of tissue from garments (without damaging them) which they inspect with a microscope to identify the fibers. But it was easier for rabbis to impose kosher inspection in the food business rather than the textile and clothing business.[160]

So we are dealing with a system established on the basis of a truncated kashruth. Consequently, arguments made in its defense, financial or otherwise, should be greeted with a fair amount of skepticism.

CHAPTER TWO

HALAL

Muslim Dietary Laws

Muslim dietary laws have evolved over time.[161]In the age of the Muhammad, the directives were rather simple. Here are the passages of the Koran which refer to this diet:

1. What is permitted (halal):

> O people! Eat of what is lawful and good on earth, and do not follow the footsteps of Satan. He is to you an open enemy. (Surat 2:168);
>
> It is He [God] who produces gardens, both cultivated and wild, and date-palms, and crops of diverse tastes, and olives and pomegranates, similar and dissimilar. Eat of its fruit when it yields... (Surat 6: 141);
>
> And the livestock—He created them for you. In them are warmth and benefits for you, and of them you eat. (Surat 16: 5);
>
> It is He Who sends down for you from the sky water. From it is drink, and with it grows vegetation for grazing. And He produces for you grains with it, and olives, and date-palms, and grapes, and all kinds of fruits. Surely in that is a sign for people who think. (Surat 16: 10-11);
>
> And it is He who made the sea to serve you, that you may eat from its tender meat... (Surat 16: 14);
>
> And there is a lesson for you in cattle: We give you a drink from their bellies, from between waste and blood, pure milk, refreshing to the drinkers. (Surat 16: 66);
>
> And your Lord inspired the bee: "Set up hives in the mountains, and in the trees, and in what they construct." Then eat of all the fruits, and go along

the pathways of your Lord, with precision. From their bellies emerges a fluid of diverse colors, containing healing for the people. Surely in this is a sign for people who reflect. (Surat 16: 68-69);

And there is a sign for them in the dead land: We give it life, and produce from it grains from which they eat. (Surat 36: 33);

2. What is forbidden (haram):

Prohibited for you are carrion, blood, the flesh of swine, and animals dedicated to other than God; also the flesh of animals strangled, killed violently, killed by a fall, gored to death, mangled by wild animals—except what you rescue, and animals sacrificed on altars. (Surat 5: 3);

O you who believe! Intoxicants [...] are abominations of Satan's doing. Avoid them, so that you may prosper. (Surat 5: 90)

Other Surats contain verses dealing with food, but the information is redundant with the above: e.g., Surat 2: 57, 60, 61; Surat 5: 1-5; Surat 6: 141-146; Surat 16: 66-68; Surat 23: 19-21; Surat 34: 15; Surat 80: 24-32. Note that everything not prohibited is permitted on principle.

What a Halal Certification Agency Says Today

The Halal Montreal Certification Agency enumerates the norms of halal on its internet site as follows:

Islam has introduced the concept of slaughter, whereby an animal would have to be properly slaughtered to be considered halal. The act of slaughtering is to ensure the quality of meat and to avoid any microbial contamination. For example, a dead but unslaughtered animal is normally associated with disease. Most diseases originate from animal's blood, therefore, slaughtering is mandatory to ensure that complete drainage of blood from the animal's body - thus minimizing the chance of microbial infection. This is consistent with the overall concept of cleanliness that is always emphasized in Islam.

All foods are considered Halal except the following:

1. Swine/pork/dog and its by-products;
2. Alcohol and intoxicants;
3. Blood and blood by-products;

4. Carnivorous animals, birds of prey and land animals without external ears;
5. Amphibious animals such as frogs, crocodiles and turtles;
6. Animals improperly slaughtered or dead before slaughtering;
7. Food contaminated with any of the above products (The Halal ingredients must not be mixed, or even come into contact with Haram materials, such as products from pig or dog, during storage, transport, cooking, serving, etc.;
8. Foods containing ingredients such as gelatin, enzymes, emulsifiers, etc. are Mushbooh or questionable.[162]

So in principle, everything that comes from the sea, milk products, cereal grains, fruits, vegetables are part of the Muslim diet and are halal. The same goes for anything one may make by combining these elements.

The Unfortunate Pig

Already present in Judaism, the ban on pork is one of the most notable prohibitions of Islam. Since pigs have a cloven hoof but do not ruminate, it is forbidden to eat their meat or even touch them. This extends to refusing any food that was in contact with pork. This tenacious prejudice against pork goes back more than a millennium and there may be several factors explaining it. The wild boar was an ancient symbol of evil. Among the ancients of the desert, pigs were perceived as dirty, lazy, eaters of trash and even of corpses and thus bearers of parasitic disease such as worms. It was clearly associated with "pollution." Such has been the teaching in mosques for centuries, although today there exists no scientific, sanitary basis for forbidding pork. But since religious principles have an absolute value, they are beyond discussion.

Yusuf al-Qaradawi, spiritual guide of the Muslim Brotherhood, founder of Qatar's first Faculty of Shari'ah and Islamic Studies[163], is famous for his broadcast *al-Shari'a wa al-Hayah*, (Sharia and Life) followed by some 60 million viewers[164]. One of his books, *The Permitted and the Prohibited in Islam*, was written around 1960 at the request of the General Institute of Islamic Culture of the University of Al-Azhar. The purpose was to provide a comprehensible book presenting Islam and its teachings for Muslims living in the United States and Europe, especially by comparing Islam to other religions. The goal was also to attract non-Muslims to Islam.[165]

He delivers a knockout blow to pork in a few lines:

> Innate nature considers it malevolent and avoids it because its favorite foods are trash and filth. Modern medicine has proven that its consumption is harmful in all climates and especially warm climates. Experience has proven that its flesh is responsible for deadly infestations of pork worm and other worms. Perhaps in the future science will uncover the secrets of this prohibition better than what we know today. The Great God has spoken the truth, for his Prophet has said: He has permitted them good things and forbidden them the bad... (al-Ar'af 7: 157).[166]

During recent years, the maintenance of the prohibition against pork has favored the growth of a new generation of halal meats: veal bacon and ham, halal pepperoni, etc. There even exists gelatin made from fish scales or algae.

"Extensible" Norms

Koranic laws reflect the daily life of desert peoples of the 7th Century, in Arabia and the entire Near East. What followed was merely a matter of interpretation and private dietary practices associated with Islam—until the 20th Century. Certain events left in their wake a terrain favorable to the future emergence of a commercial halal label. First, the advent of the politico-religious Sunni movement known as the Muslim Brotherhood, founded in Egypt in 1928. To this day they preach the establishment of regimes that apply Sharia (Islamic Law). During the Second World War and the years that followed, the American government employed (especially in Munich) certain Muslim Brotherhood members to whom funds were allotted for the struggle against the "great communist enemy," the Soviet Union.[167] With its oil revenue, Wahhabi Saudi Arabia, beginning in 1975, gave out billions of dollars every year to propagate radical Sunni Islam in the world.[168] Another notable fact was the establishment of the Islamic Republic of Iran by the Ayatollah Khomeini in 1979.

The arrival of the concept of halal certification coincided with the emergence of religious fundamentalism. It must also be said that the concept was facilitated by the precedent set decades earlier in the United States when Joseph Jacobs got the idea of having commonly consumed items certified by rabbis, and the well-established system that grew out of this.

As with kosher, the challenge was to connect a literal reading of religious texts (not taking into account the context in which they were written) with the stunning diversity of contemporary grocery products. After all, Allah was not able to forbid men of the 7th Century products unknown at the time.

According to Hajj Habib Ghanim, President of the USA Halal Chamber of Commerce and Director of Halal Certification at the Islamic Society of the Washington Area (ISWA):

> The introduction of halal certification to the United States owes much to the kosher certifiers who conducted similar, well-established activity and know the industry. We have learned from them. We have excellent relations with agencies such as Star-K and others because of the similarities…. We are learning from our Jewish cousins who have been operating for years. We are learning, and we have a great deal of support from them.[169]

In Canada, the food processing plant Al-Safa Halal (burgers, chicken nuggets) was founded in 1999 by David Muller, an Orthodox Jew. In 2008 he sold his shares in the company.[170] And in France, the Halal brand Isla Délice was launched in 1991 by the Jewish businessman Jean-David Hertzog.[171]

Arrival of Halal in the United States: Under the Sign of the Muslim Brotherhood

The concept of halal certification in the United States goes back to the mid-60s. It presents itself as a security measure for Muslims living in non-Muslim countries "allowing them to preserve their identity and respect their religious obligations."[172] Its vanguard was the Muslim Student Association of the US and Canada (MSA), created in 1963, of whom three of the founders[173] belonged to the Muslim Brotherhood. Financed and directed from Riyadh in Saudi Arabia, this "student association" was the first vehicle for promoting Wahhabi ideology in the United States. Among its demands are prayer rooms and halal meals on campus.

In 1982, the MSA and three other organizations founded the Islamic Society of North America (ISNA), which offered halal certification services.[174] Several of its members have belonged to the Muslim Brotherhood.[175]

In 2007 the New York police department determined that the MSA was an incubator of Islamic radicalization. MSA's tactics amounted to a kind of furtive jihad made up of non-violent initiatives with a long-term aim of imposing sharia over the entire world in a non-conflictual manner. Under cover of tolerance and personal rights, this furtive jihad is introducing the elements of sharia one by one into Western society and then demanding non-Muslims accept it. It is a strategy similar to the one described in an internal Muslim Brotherhood document *An Explanatory Memorandum on the General Strategic Goal for the Group in North America*, which listed MSA among 29 friendly organizations with the goal of destroying the United States and making it into an Islamic nation. These groups teach Muslims that "their mission in America is a sort of great jihad aiming to destroy Western civilization from within and sabotage its miserable dwelling using its own hands [...] in order that [...] God's religion [Islam] wins out over all other religions."[176]

The MSA appears to be very close to several extreme left political activist groups such as the Black Radical Congress, the Free Palestine Alliance, the Kensington Welfare Rights Union, the Korea Truth Commission, the Mexico Solidarity Network, the Nicaragua Network, the Young Communist League, and the young People's Socialist League. At the beginning of the 2000s, the MSA was an influential member of the orientation committee of International ANSWER, a front of the Marxist-Leninist Workers World Party. Certain local chapters of the MSA are signatories of a February 20, 2002 document written by the group Refuse & Resist, a front for the Revolutionary Communist Party.[177]

But "furtive jihad" is hardly confined to our neighbors to the south.

Halal Certification in Canada: Under Saudi Control

Halal certification in Canada is relatively recent. Founded in 1963, the Muslim Student Association of the US and Canada[178], tied to the Muslim Brotherhood[179], offers various community services. Succeeding to the MSA, ISNA (The Islamic Society of North America—Canada) is the first organization to offer certification services for food products made or processed in Canada. It was courtesy of ISNA that the first halal slaughterhouse was certified in 1990, the Maple Lodge Farms company.[180] It offers a range of products under the brand name Zabiha Halal.

The industrial scale system of halal production thus put into operation was nothing less than a result of direct foreign interference in the Canadian food industry. Indeed, for Maple Lodge Farms[181] to be able to offer halal certified products, it was subject to several inspection tours by "Islamic scholars, experts and veterinarians" from the Wahhabi organization[182] Dar-ul-Ifta in Riyadh, Saudi Arabia[183].

Dar-ul-Ifta is in fact the Permanent Committee for Scholarly Research and Ifta [deliverance of fatwas, or Islamic legal decisions or decrees] of Saudi Arabia's Wahhabi Sunnites. We are speaking of such fatwas as the sentence of 10 years in prison and 1000 lashes imposed on Saudi blogger Raïf Badawi for having expressed himself freely[184], or the decapitations by sword for various "crimes" such as wanting to leave the Muslim religion (apostasy)[185]. The highest religious authority of Saudi Arabia was at the origin of certifying the first halal slaughterhouse in Canada.

So, as Jacques Godbout has written regarding an essay by the Algerian novelist and engineer Boualem Sansal, "governing in Allah's name means imposing sharia and returning to medieval practices, Koranic Law being by definition incompatible with democracy, which allows people the freedom to speak and act. [...] To avoid losing their thrones, the oil kings, who want no democracy, covertly encourage war on the West. Saudi Arabia subsidizes mosques as far away as Canada."[186] And subsidizes militant Islam all the way to our plates?

In 2007 the Islamic Food and Nutrition Council of Canada (IFANCC)[187] was incorporated in English-speaking Canada as a nonprofit organization "dedicated to scientific research in the domain of nutrition, food and health in the services of the food industry and Muslim consumers." The IFANCC now sells halal certification in English speaking Canada and has been supervising Maple Lodge Farms since November 1, 2013.[188] The corporate website of Zabiha Halal notes that the slaughterhouse is also approved "by numerous other Imams and Islamic organizations such as Dr. Mohammad Iqbal Alnadvi of Sharia Consulting Services, the Fiqh Council of North America, Imam Hamid Slimi of the Syeda Khadijah Center, the Islamic Centre of Canada, the Association musulmane des commerces de viandes halal du Québec, the Masjid Istiqlal-Indonesia Mosque, the municipalities of the United Arab Emirates, and numerous other Muslim organizations well-known over the entire world.[189] Note that the Fiqh Council of North America is an organ of the International Union of Muslim Scholars, the clerical wing of the Muslim Brotherhood.[190]

The largest chicken slaughterhouse in Canada (halal or otherwise), Maple Lodge Farms is a great industrial establishment that operates at a rapid tempo. For halal, the birds are hung upside down by their claws, put into a neck stretcher aligned with a rotating blade, and slaughtered in the presence of a Muslim cleric who pronounces a blessing "in the name of Allah the Greatest."

According to the organization Mercy for Animals, this factory is a real "house of horrors." A worker who infiltrated the slaughter line in 2015 reports that "it is hell on earth," and that he had never seen such a level of abuse in a slaughterhouse, both in transportation, manipulation and the process for slaughtering birds. The company had to pay a fine of $80,000 in 2013 for having left birds to die of cold during transportation. In the light of recent hidden-camera images collected by this employee, Mercy for Animals is considering bringing further accusations of animal cruelty against Maple Lodge Farms.[191]

Nevertheless, Maple Lodge Farms is doing very good business, since it is the "officially halal" chicken supplier for Loblaws which operates under various names and owns or controls 1049 retail outlets in the country. In Quebec, its names are Loblaws, Maxi & Cie, Provigo, Club Entrepôt, Intermarché, and Axep. And, as required by globalization, Zabiha Halal products are exported to 50 countries.

Halal Without Borders

Once companies reach a certain scale of production, it is not surprising that some of them wish to carve out a place for themselves among Canadian and international monopolies. Globalization has a leverage effect on the development of the halal market, estimated at about $700 billion per year. In 2009, Canadian export of halal food products amounted to $2,906,291,433. Saudi Arabia is the biggest customer.[192] In 2010, Canada exported $3.2 billion in US dollars of halal products. In 2013, Canada sold $15.2 million beef products to the Gulf States of Bahrain, Kuwait, Oman, Qatar, Saudi Arabia and the United Arab Emirates.[193] Écolait, headquartered near Terrebonne in Quebec, is one of the largest slaughterhouses in the country, with an annual production of 100,000 calves; 3-5% of their revenue of $100 million comes from the sale of halal products in North America, Saudi Arabia, Jordan, Egypt, Dubai, Oman, and even Japan.[194] There have been cases of foreign capital coming into Quebec to reinforce the implantation of the halal label. We may cite the halal slaughterhouse of Louis Lafrance et Fils Ltée of Grand-Mère, which was bought for $4 million in 2012 by Africa Suppliers[195], an international consulting firm in Niger[196] active in the meat market. The director of the slaughterhouse comes from the African oil industry.[197] According to the authors of a university study, "there is a rumor to the effect that foreign, specifically Qatari, capital is looking for agricultural land in Quebec to set up livestock companies, while a production line controlled by Quebec citizens of Black African origin is trying to establish itself."[198] The halal slaughterhouse Viandes Richelieu, located at Massueville in Quebec, is one of the principle furnishers of horsemeat to France.[199] The slaughter of horses is illegal in the United States, so the majority of the animals come from our southern neighbor. Following an investigation, the association Éthique & Animaux reported mistreatment of horses in the course of transportation and slaughter in 2012[200], revelations which lead some European businesses to stop selling Viandes Richelieu products[201].

As for the domestic halal market in Canada, it amounted to $1.9 billion in 2010.

Halal Certifiers active in Quebec

There are no trustworthy statistics measuring the percentage of strict believers or practitioners among the roughly 300,000 Muslims in Quebec. Estimates hover around 10%.[202] Purchasers of halal products do not necessarily belong to that community, especially as concerns the meat trade.

At least seven organizations sell halal certification in Quebec. Some of them are small private enterprises not associated with any particular mosque or Imam. According to the business register of Quebec's provincial government, the Halal Montreal Certification Authority Inc. specializes in "analysis and certification of halal products, distribution of halal products."[203] This for-profit company based in Quebec and Detroit Michigan says it is recognized[204] by JAKIM (Jabatan Kemajuan Islam Malaysia) and by MUIS, and is a member of the IHI Alliance (International Halal Integrity Alliance) as well as the WHFC (World Halal Food Council). It is active across Canada. The HMCA logo is found on products as diverse as frozen blueberries, fish gelatin, zinc oxide and, of course, meats.

The Aboubakkerseddik Cultural Center, within which exists the Abou Bakr Asseddique Mosque under the direction of Imam Habib Marzougui, is home to the Association des viandes halal (AVH), which states that it operates in the domain of "overseeing and inspecting the slaughter of sheep." The Olymel company's chicken is certified by AVH, which collects tens of thousands of dollars a year in this way.[205] The Abou Bakr Asseddique Mosque, the Aboubakkerseddik Cultural Center, and the Association des viandes halal are located in a building on Jean-Talon Street, Montreal, that belongs to the Muslim Association of Canada (MAC). On its website, MAC states that it takes inspiration from the Islamist movement and the Muslim Brotherhood.[206] The Royal Canadian Mounted Police discovered that between 2001 and 2010, this organization gave $297,000 to the International Relief Fund for the Afflicted and Needy (IRFAN), a "charity" which collects funds for Hamas[207], which has been considered a terrorist organization by Canada since 2002[208]. The website Pointe de bascule sounded the alarm about this matter in 2014[209]; it was later picked up by La Presse on the basis of exclusive documents obtained by the Royal Mounted Police. "For years, the Islamist group Hamas has enjoyed a very active infrastructure of terrorist financing in Montreal, which has solicited Muslim individuals and organizations under cover of charitable activity.[210] [...] In April 2011 the Canadian Revenue Agency revokes IRFAN's status as a charity after determining that the organization had transferred $14.6 million to Hamas during the period 2005-2009 alone. On April 24, 2014, Public Safety Canada added IRFAN-Canada to its list of banned terrorist organization.[211] Notably, AVH certifies the Olymel and Louis Lafrance slaughterhouses.

In Sherbrooke, the Service abattages et viandes halal de l'oasis company is active according to the Quebec Business Register in the domain of "Halal slaughter and sale of meat." It certifies as halal the products of the Viandes Giroux company.[212] Another company is based at the same address, Solution Informatique. Thus, in a single apartment located above a bakery there are based two for-profit companies: a halal certification agency and a computer support service.

Canada Halal Examination & Certification (CHEC) certifies the cheese products of two Quebec companies as well as two meat plants.[213] On its corporate site, the agency clearly indicates that halal is tied to sharia.[214]

Based in Mississauga, Ontario, the Islamic Society of North America-Canada (ISNA Canada) certifies food and even pharmaceutical products through its division the Halal Certification Agency (HCA). Among the certified companies in Quebec we may cite Les Aliments Edelweiss, the veal slaughterhouse Écolait as well as Duchesnay and its prescription medication Diclectin. According to the Toronto Sun, "documents in possession of the US Justice Department on the financing of Hamas indicate that the Islamic Society of North America (ISNA) has played a key role in diffusing the doctrine of the Muslim Brotherhood. ISNA-USA figures among the 29 most important members and affiliates listed by the Brotherhood. Although the Mississauga branch in Ontario claims it operates independently of the umbrella organization based in Indiana, it has had and still has administrators also sitting on the council of ISNA-USA, besides using its name and logo. "[215]

According to a text published by the Journal de Montréal in 2015, "FBI documents mention that the Central American branch of ISNA is a creation of the Muslim Brotherhood and has contributed to financing Hamas."[216]

A January 22, 2015 report by La Presse informed us that in September 2013 the Canadian Revenue Agency had revoked the charitable status of ISNA's fundraising division. "Investigations led CRA to believe that the organization took part in a financing strategy along with the Kashmiri Canadian Council/Kashmiri Relief Fund of Canada (KCC/KRFC), donors not recognized by the law whose only aim was to send funds to a Pakistani NGO called the Relief Organization for Kashmiri Muslims (ROKM)," as we read in CRA's brief report. In sum, the tax agency reproaches the ISNA development Foundation with having sent $282,000 to Jamaat-al-Islami. The armed division of this Pakistani organization, Hizbul Mujahideen, is recognized as a terrorist organization by the European Union. It seeks to create an Islamic State in Indian Kashmir.[217]

The Islamic Food and Nutrition Council of Canada (IFANCA), the Halal Monitoring Authority, and À votre service (AVS)[218] are other certification agencies active in Quebec. The certification sector being very lucrative it should be no surprise to witness the arrival of new competitors.

From Halal to Sharia

There is indeed an Islamic plan to conquer the world (jihad).[219] The former deputy of the Liberal Party of Quebec, Fatima Houda-Pépin, known for her courageous opposition to Islamic fundamentalism, defines it as follows:

It is a political ideology disguised as a religion. The fundamentalists want to change society so that it is governed according to their own principles, their own not necessarily religious values. They use religion to attain their goals. For them, democracy is the enemy. It must be defeated, because its laws do not follow their principles or the path of God.[220]

In December 2010, Mustafa Ceric, the Grand Mufti of Bosnia and Herzegovina, declared in a speech to the 1st Global Halal Congress in Islamabad, Pakistan, that one must "conquer the world via the halal movement"[221]—a sinister echo recalling the Nazi Thousand Year Reich project: Heute Deutschland, morgen die Welt! (Today Germany, tomorrow the world!).

Sign of the times? Published on February 23, 2016, a United Nations report aptly titled "*From niche to mainstream: Halal Goes Global*" states that the "halal trend" is unescapable. Islamic fundamentalism have found in neoliberal capitalism its perfect match. In fact, it's a radically different set of values than those of the Western civilization that's being surreptitiously exported around the globe. A wide range of multinationals reap profit out of that "business of gullibility". The phantasmal "Sharia-law way of life" is presented as THE new cool, such as seen in the modest fashion trend. Hijabi models in haute couture catwalks (Tommy Hilfiger, Marc Jacobs, Dolce & Gabbana, Michael Kors, Lanvin, Fendi, Burberry, Valentino etc.) as well as in Cover Girl or L'Oréal Paris makeup ads, Olympic athletes promoting Nike burkinis, new veiled Barbie dolls, halal food, travel and accommodation, etc. The "Sharia-compliant" products and services sector grows bigger every year. Western economies partake in it. As for the sea of suffering brought into the real world by Islam's totalitarian ideology, it is entirely evacuated.

Everyday Sharia

Sharia is a sort of legal code which governs all aspects of religious, social, political and individual life. For Muslims, it is the path that leads to happiness in the life here below and in the other world. It was codified in a law book based on the classic sources of Islam, which are the Koran (containing Allah's revelation transmitted by the angel Gabriel to Muhammad between 612 and 632 AD)[222], the hadiths[223] and the Sunna[224] relating the words and actions of the prophet or his companions. Entitled Umdat al-Salik, the manual of Islamic Holy Law was written by Ahmad

64

ibn Naqib al-Misri (1302-1367), whose contemporary version and English translation have been approved by the celebrated al-Azhar University in Egypt, and, in the United States, by the International Institute of Islamic Thought.

Sharia is divided into two parts: concerning worship and concerning human interaction. The first part contains the Five Pillars of Islam:

1. The declaration of Faith (There is no God but God, and Muhammad is his Prophet);
2. Prayer five times per day;
3. Obligatory alms and charity;
4. The Ramadan fast (abstaining from eating, drinking, smoking and sexual relations from dawn to sunset);
5. The Great Pilgrimage, at least once in one's life.

The second part contains rules relating to:

1. Financial transactions and donations;
2. Rules of inheritance;[225]
3. Marriage, divorce, and custody of children;
4. Food and drink (including hunting and the rules for the ritual slaughter of animals);
5. War and peace;
6. Criminal infractions (all the way to decapitation);
7. Judicial affairs (including witnesses and evidence).[226]

Sharia is also strongly discriminatory against women[227], homosexuals, unbelievers and apostates, as witnessed by the notion of uncleanness, the a'yan najisah (things intrinsically unclean). According to Islamic Law, there are nine of these:

1. Urine
2. Excrement
3. Sperm
4. Blood
5. Corpses
6. Dogs
7. Pigs
8. Kafirs [non-Muslims]
9. Intoxicating drinks[228]

Radio Canada reports that in certain Canadian towns blind persons and their seeing-eye dogs are increasingly refused by taxi-drivers, particularly for "religious reasons."[229]

The website muslimvillage.com has published an article entitled "*Sharia in Australia, Already a Reality*" by Sally Neighbour, citing the secretary of the Australian Islamic Mission, Siddiq Buckley: "There are examples of [sharia] practices already in place. We have Muslim schools, mosques, funeral salons, stores and companies. We have slaughterhouses, Islamic charitable institutions, Islamic financial institutions. There are so many things—halal meals served by airline companies. All this forms part of sharia."[230] A situation which as a whole is nearly the same in several Western countries.

The European Court of Human Rights determined July 31, 2001 that sharia was incompatible with democracy and the Universal Declaration of Human Rights. This decree was confirmed by the Grand Chamber of that court on February 13, 2003.

Doing Both a Thing and Its Opposite

Officially committed to the struggle against radicalization, what is Canada and the US doing in regard to this sinister sharia which the jihadis dream of imposing on the entire world? Answer: sharia is an integral part of our economic system. The Dow Jones has a sharia-compliant S&P Index.[231] The Toronto stock exchange also has a sharia-compliant index (TSX 60 Shariah).[232] Sixty-six financial companies in North America are involved in activities tied to the shariah-compliant financial sector, and not the least of them, including Bank of America, Barclays, Bloomberg, BNP Paribas, JP Morgan Chase, CitiBank, Crédit Suisse, Deutsche Bank, Goldman Sachs, HSBC, Merrill Lynch and Morgan Stanley.[233] It is Toronto's ambition to become the largest Islamic financial center in North America. The first Islamic Bank is about to open in Canada.[234]

In France, "even mortgage loans must respect sharia, because for Muslims, Islamic law has greater authority than French law."[235] Switzerland is fifteenth in the world in sharia-compliant financial activities.[236] Many Canadian companies offer sharia compliant financial products.[237] Halal mortgages have been offered in Canada for the past 30 years with the complete acceptance of our government.

In Quebec, the office of Montreal notary Chalati offers a "Notarized Last Will & Testament" service according to Islamic law. There are organizations offering Islamic mortgages[238], marriages[239], funeral services and burials[240]. From infancy until death, the possibility of leading a life conformable to the principles of sharia is a fait accompli in Canada.

Islamization and the Role of Halal

There are several steps in a society's Islamization, including the introduction of:

1. Wearing the veil for women and girls; in the extreme case, the burkini[241] in public pools;
2. Prayer rooms in schools and companies;
3. Halal norms in the food business and special meals in nursery schools, cafeterias and prison in order to habituate the population to allowing such practices;
4. Religious schools to assure new cadres;
5. Muslim ethnic enclaves;
6. Legal action to intimidate critics of Islam.

Facilitated by the powerful support of kosher labels, the quiet implantation of halal procedures on Canadian soil nearly thirty years ago by Wahhabi, Salafist or Khomeinist agents has opened the Pandora's box of sharia. The following passages taken from the corporate site of Halal Montreal Certification Authority are conclusive:

> The location, the material and equipment are cleaned in accordance with sharia law; [...] At the time of slaughter, the trachea (respiratory passage, halqum) and esophagus (passage for food and water) must be cut in conformity with sharia law; the phrase "in Allah's name" (Bismillah) must be pronounced as the animal is being slaughtered. [..] The HMCA will deliver a certificate of halal slaughter to any applicant they deem apt for slaughtering animals in conformity with sharia law.[242]

The website of a Quebec regional slaughterhouse also uses a wording that could not be clearer:

Since 1999, Viandes Giroux 1997 Inc. has been slaughtering cattle according to halal norms. A certifier from the East Angus factory in the Eastern Townships makes sure the slaughter procedures respect sharia law. We serve a clientele which demands halal certification. Our certification allows us to assure the conformity of products in the spirit of Islam, whose objective is to define hygienic rules and respect for the animal and the environment.[243]

A first halal slaughterhouse for cattle has recently appeared on Prince Edward Island.[244] The Atlantic beef Products company is supervised by the Islamic Food and Nutrition Council of Canada (IFANCC)[245], whose Religious Affairs Committee is directed by Dr. Iqbal Masood Nadvi, a doctor in sharia law who taught for several years in Saudi Arabia[246]. IFANCC offers certification services to companies such as Campbell's, Cavendish Farms, Délices Al-Manar, DuPont, McCain, Petro-Canada, and Saputo, just to name a few.[247]

Canonical Muslim law has, then, already been implanted in part of Canada, as well as in other Western countries. So we should not be surprised that a certain share of Muslim immigration demands halal meat as soon as they arrive in the country. At the beginning of 2016, Syrian refugees settled in New Brunswick made urgent demands to this effect.[248] Local merchants were instantly burning to satisfy them. In Alberta, the halal food bank run by the Muslim Families Network accommodated the new arrivals in one of their annual distributions.[249] And since then illegal immigrants crossing the Canadian border are being offered religious meals. The effort to adapt is born by the receiving country which, whether unconsciously or through a tragic ignorance, signal that elements of Islamic law can prevail.

Grey Zones

According to the study *Les enjeux de la viande halal au Québec* ["The Stakes of Halal Meat in Quebec"], contribution to a collective volume published by Presses de l'Université Laval in 2014, there is no consensus among halal actors. Halal norms vary according to national and ethnic factors along with the Sunnite/Shiite division found in the Near East and Pakistan. So the "disagreements among Muslim butchers, grocers and meat wholesalers are as much commercial as religious. At the center of it all is the revenue from certification. Any group which succeeds in mobilizing enough merchants to create a Quebec halal certification agency will have access to a significant source of revenue."[250] Notably, there is disagreement over the issue of stunning animals before slaughter.

"The stakes of the halal market in Quebec as elsewhere are first of all financial and, secondly, socio-religious,"[251] say the authors of the study. For the financial attraction will kindle more than just intracommunal rivalries. Agribusiness and the large chain supermarkets have noticed this promising market. A 2009 article which appeared in Alfa, the newspaper of the North African community, tells us a lot about the racketeering that prevails in this domain. It emphasizes especially the anarchic character of the halal meat business.[252] The big retail outlets (IGA, Intermarché, Loblaws, Maxi, Metro, Provigo and Wal-Mart) increasingly compete over small halal butcheries by using a loss leader pricing strategy to attract Muslim customers. They "can offer halal meat at competitive prices because they have sufficient working capital to lower the price of halal meat by 50% on occasion and make up the same amount on other products they offer."[253] Might this mean on all other kinds of articles (milk products, fruits, vegetables, grains, beverages, soaps, etc.)? In that case, it seems the customer base as a whole is making up for losses due to halal meats in our supermarkets.

In the end, the supermarket chains sell halal meat cheek by jowl with refrigerated containers containing pork and wine, details which will not deter Muslim customers in search of good deals.

Are You Buying Halal Meat Without Knowing It?

Customers in general are subsidizing the loss leader pricing fixed by the supermarkets. According to some sources, they may also purchase halal meat unknowingly, indirectly absorbing agribusinesses' costs of halal certification. A public affairs program of 2012 revealed that "all Olymel chickens from Saint-Damase are slaughtered according to Muslim rites. But depending on the company, this fact need not be indicated on the package. "It isn't necessary," opines Richard Vigneault, spokesman for Olymel, because "it does not change the product in any way."[254]

The industrial process does, however, have an intrusive and discriminatory character: The Halal Meat Association which issues certificates of authenticity, demands that Muslim employees participate every day in the work of slaughter. "These people were required to put someone in charge of the machine before starting it up, to pronounce the name of Allah and to employ two or three persons after the slaughter to verify if the animal was correctly slaughtered," explains the Association's founder, Abdelhamid Aouchiche. There are even three Muslim inspectors busy making unannounced visits to slaughterhouses to make sure the process is being respected, conditions accepted by the slaughterhouses which sign the contract. Olymel's spokesman "did not specify how much money was paid to the Muslim Association. But he acknowledged paying "thousands of dollars" every year, money collected by the directors of the Abou Bakr Essedik Mosque on Jean-Talon Street in Montreal [presided over by Imam Mohamad Habib Marzougui]: "We control most of the halal chicken trade in Quebec," declares the Imam, who collects annual and monthly fees from certified slaughterhouses.[255] Note that Olymel slaughters nearly 750,000 chickens per week at Saint-Damase, and also owns the brands Flamingo and Lafleur.

Viandes Métropolitain of Montreal's distributor, Samih Bahsoun, explains that to reduce costs, slaughterhouses which produce halal meat convert their entire system of production. In 2004, Mr. Bahsoun convinced the former directors of the Avicomax slaughterhouse of Drummondville to turn exclusively to Islamic manual slaughter. "They put on a halal label where necessary, but all their chickens are halal. It costs less to do it this way. That's the way it is in most slaughterhouses which practice halal."[256] In 2010, Avicomax sold 40% of its poultry production in the standard, non-Muslim market.[257] A former owner once declared: "obviously, our resale cost is higher because of the way the animals are slaughtered" [by hand and facing East].[258] With nearly 200,000 chickens slaughtered per week, Avicomax serves customers such as Maxi and Loblaws.[259]

This discreet overflow into the conventional market is not something recent. A market study carried out by the Provincial Government of Alberta in January 2005 revealed that "no less than 15% of all cattle slaughtered were processed in halal-certified establishments." A large part of this meat, often processed, necessarily finds its way to the plates of non-Muslims without their knowing it. In Quebec, 30% of the meat coming from animal killed in the kosher or halal ways get into the mainstream market.[260]

How much is paid to the certifiers per kilo? Although we have no exact figures, it is known that the halal certifier IFANCA Canada demands 22 cents per kilo of beef.[261] Only a public inquiry could reveal the total sum of payments received annually by the various certifiers operating in the country.

A Lack of Transparency

In 2011 the federal government of Canada looked into the possibility of subjecting halal production to mandatory labeling, but it did not carry this out.[262] In 2013, the Canadian Food Inspection Agency (CFIA) announced a consulting period of 75 days regarding a project for regulating halal labeling. "The regulation would have forbid using the world halal, an Arabic letter or any other word, expression, illustration, sign, symbol, mark or other representation on a food product label indicating or creating the impression that the product is halal unless the name of the organization or person who certified the product halal is also indicated on the label." The CFIA also announced that "it would not establish any norm for certifying food products halal and would offer no approval to certification agencies because of the absence of consensus among the interested parties on any common set of halal norms."[263]

Bouazza Mache of the MarkEthnik marketing agency told Le Soleil newspaper that "it is not the role of CFIA to determine who can certify production processes." He admits that the regulation as proposed would not allow non-Muslims to know whether the product they are buying was produced according to Islamic rules. In the case of meat, e.g., these rules require that the animal be slaughtered without having been stunned beforehand, a practice shocking to some people.[264]

In 2014, the Canadian Food Inspection Agency (CFIA) ruled that "any claim to being 'halal' figuring on a food product, wrapper, or in advertising must henceforward be accompanied by the name of the certification agency," but it did not require producers to label their products halal.[265]

Out of the Mountain Came a Mouse

Can this resistance to labeling be explained by the fear of possible boycotts on the part of consumers? And the necessity of raising the price of duly blessed meats that might follow? One thing is certain: anarchy continues to prevail and the profits are gratifying to the interested parties. But what happens to the revenue earned from certification on the pretext of religion? And to the revenue of companies or shops owned by Muslims?

71

The Muslim Tax

Unlike in Catholicism, where being extremely rich is often frowned upon[266], Islam values personal wealth on the express condition that the believer respect the third pillar of Islam which consists in paying the zakat, a form of tax that every good Muslim must pay. But the zakat must not be confused with charity and alms, which are voluntary. The zakat is obligatory. There are two kinds of zakat. The zakat al-Fitre consists in giving about two pounds of food to the needy during Ramadan. And then there is the zakat al maal which we will be concerned with here.[267] On this subject, one may consult the reporting form for the Muslim tax from the Islamic Society of North America—Canada (ISNA Canada), which gives a good idea of it.

Each lunar year, every practicing Muslim is supposed to pay a tax of 2.5% on most of his possessions. In fact, it amounts to a 'flat' or proportional tax.[268] Just what is taxed? The goods concerned include cash, bank accounts, precious metals, jewels, income, profits and salaries. Although there may be various interpretations and nuances[269], in principle there are eight authorized uses for the zakat:

1 To give to the poor;
2 To give to those in want;
3 To pay collectors who work for an Imam or for an Islamic State[270];
4 To give to new converts;
5 To redeem Muslim slaves;
6 To give to those in debt;
7 To give for the cause of God;
8 To give to the traveler in distress to permit him to return home.[271]

In principle, the zakat cannot be used for anything else. We must pay special attention to point 7, whose meaning is as follows: "The cause of God principally includes holy war (used, e.g., for equipment, supplies, etc.) but also anything of public utility such as the construction of hospitals, dispensaries, the purchase of furniture for mosques. But all this being said, holy war enjoys priority."[272] Now, fighting for Allah implies fighting his enemies. In other words, it can mean "financing jihadist terror."[273]

In non-Muslim countries, Imams manage the sums collected, whether by zakat, charity, alms or gifts. They do so either directly or through nonprofit organizations created for the purpose. They dispose of the money as they please and, as concerns zakat funds, they can under certain conditions assign them to purposes other than the eight prescribed. In certain cases, if the payer has specified or given permission, or in cases of a budget surplus, the amount collected can be allotted to upkeep of the mosque, the purchase of computers or of books to teach the Koran to children, etc.[274]

But this system of offerings opens the door to fiscal fraud, e.g., by giving out inflated receipts to generate tax refunds under cover of paying zakat, or donating to charity, or simply under false pretenses. This is what has happened at the Islamic Society of North America—Canada (ISNA Canada):

> In 2010, the director Mohammad Ashraf was caught with his hand in the cookie jar in the course of an audit carried out by a certified accountant. He gave out fraudulent receipts under such false pretenses as repayment of student loans, funerals held at his mosque, transferring funds from certification agencies to a secret personal account, etc. In the case of transferring funds, he issued himself a receipt as if he had made a personal donation to ISNA Canada. His mosque's total annual revenue amounted to nearly $1 million. But in four years, only $196,460 were used to aid impoverished Muslims.[275]

No charges were ever brought against Mohammad Ashraf. ISNA Canada is the very organization which in 1990, with the aid of Saudi Arabia, became the first to offer certification for halal products made or processed in Canada. We may well ask how many millions have thus been able to pass through the books of this agency and mosque in the course of some thirty years when Ashraf presided over the Muslim community of Mississauga. And of these millions, how many went to serve dubious goals?

The mere idea that there may exist at present a world system of Islamic tax collection is enough to be worrisome. Is the web of a great Islamic Caliphate being discreetly woven at this very moment?

Irrational Prohibitions Converted into Global Business Opportunities

For the 1.5 billion Muslims on the planet, the lucrative market in halal products amounted to $1.12 trillion (US) in 2014. According to the *State of the Global Islamic Economy Report 2015/16*, this market will attain $3.75 trillion (US) in 2020.[276]

Far from limiting itself to meat, halal certifications cover an astronomical range of foods, drinks, medications, cosmetics, personal hygiene and household products, raw materials, and industrial equipment and services. Even cat food!

According to the Koran, Allah created everything on earth for human use, all is halal (permitted) except what He declared haram (forbidden).[277] Forbidden foods are pork and derived products, alcohol, intoxicating substances and animals which have not been slaughtered in accord with Muslim rites. On this last point, the President of the Islamic Food and Nutrition Council of America stated in 2006 that there exists no unanimity: "because of the absence of central authority and the multiple divisions within the Muslim religion, halal norms are not uniform. At the extreme, some Imams or Islamic centers hold that an animal must not be stunned and must be held down manually, as was done 1400 years ago.[278]

So, anything is intrinsically halal unless it can be proven otherwise. The problem is that certifiers only operate under the converse principle: all which is not certified halal is haram. This violates Allah's commandment, which states: "Do not declare haram the good things which Allah has made halal for you."[279]

The plethora of Islamic fatwas (juridical opinions)[280] and fiqh (elements of jurisprudence)[281] relating to the interpretation of dietary rules[282] along with variable opinions[283] and practices within different Muslim communities bear witness to the extent of disagreement. Now, these decrees have a merely relative authority. And there are many schools or *madhab* (paths) *of fiqh*, both among Sunnis and among Shias.

Note that 90% of Muslims are Sunnis and that the Shiites are divided into several currents. The word Sunni comes from sunna (rules of God)[284], and represent the line of conduct of Mohamad, final prophet of Islam. His acts and words, as well as those of his companions, are intrinsically valid and recorded in various collections called hadith.[285]

Sharia (Islamic Law) is partly founded on hadiths, but Shiites and Sunnis do not agree on the validity of the same hadiths. This creates variants in religious traditions and jurisprudence.

Halal is merely a word that means permitted, and owes entirely to Sharia its status as a precept.

The Alliance Between Neoliberalism
and Religious Fundamentalism

The bidding war between dietary norms from archaic and barbarous traditions (as exposed in the hadiths) finds the setting of its dreams in globalization[286], and not merely for Imams attracted by the collection of fees on halal meat. While extremists will see an unhoped-for chance to implant discreetly one aspect of sharia, others will simply see an opportunity to make a lot of money. The industry did not wait for Muslims to come to agreement among themselves: halal certification made its debut in 1980. Merchants succeeded in imposing the principal of a commercial definition of halal even as Islamic jurists, the competent intellectual authorities in religious terms, continue to dispute the meaning of halal. Here is an excerpt from the investigative report *Halal à tous les étals* by Michael Turin:

> Fethallah Otmani, spokesman for the AVS certification agency (considered hardline) which inspects slaughterhouses to ensure that halal meat is really halal, explains: "Companies have become aware of the impact of the world 'halal.'" This is mere marketing now, he exclaims. For him, there is nothing religious about any of it. These operations create an additional line of demarcation from other, non-Muslim consumers, he notes. French companies, conscious or not of encouraging discriminatory consumerism, have seen in the dietary prohibitions of the Muslim religion a splendid commercial opportunity. Marketing operations have made use of sectarian prohibitions as sales arguments. The companies quickly understood that the mention of halal would reassure consumers and get them to buy.[287]

Florence Bergeaud-Blackler, sociologist and researcher at IREMAM (Institute of Research and Study on the Arab and Muslim World) of Aix-en-Provence, wrote in her book *Comprendre le halal*:

> Halal has been able to develop because a liberal globalist model of consumption has triumphed. Every halal product is an Islamic version of a local product: it has no country, no origin, no color. Halal is a guarantee that the product was made under conditions which exclude all contact with pork or alcohol and (if it is a meat product) that the animal was slaughtered according to a Muslim rite. But there are plenty of such rites![288] The halal market is a marketing invention, something that

embarrasses many Muslim authorities who find the whole situation a mare's nest.[289]

Slaughter and certification only bring substantial sums to mosques which succeed in maintaining oversight. The most important halal certifier in Europe, Bruno Bernard, is not even a Muslim! Even the great multinationals like Nestlé and Campbell's have jumped on the halal train. Florence Bergeaud-Blackler indicates that the Imams have serious competitors:

> The industrial scale halal market was born in the 1980s on the basis of guarantees by ordinary Muslim slaughterers or those of embassies or supervisors sent by the importing countries. Kosher certification is attached to rabbinical authorities, while halal certificates are sold by commercial companies which need not render any account to a religious authority. From this recent history it follows that if the concept "halal" belongs to the intellectual domain of Islam, its industrial version has been perfected by businessmen, and that as a consequence the "halal market" belongs largely to them. And they have no intention of doing away with "a tax" on the Muslim religion.[290]

As Michel Turin writes: "The halal trade offers consumers an incredible quantity of products in stupefying assortment such as does not exist in any country of North Africa or the Near East." According to Philippe Lawson, in Muslim countries, "the question of certification does not even arise. [But] Muslim countries that want to import products from industrialized countries want to be certain that they are produced according to Koranic principles."[291] So Egypt and Saudi Arabia "send representatives to Canadian slaughterhouses to assure themselves that halal slaughter is being practiced there according to their requirements."[292]

One Imam's Vehement Denunciation of Halal Certification

Revolted by the existence of halal certification, Imam Habib Bewley of the Jumu'a Mosque in Cape Town, South Africa, vehemently denounced in one of his sermons what he called "the fiasco of halal certification." To understand his frustration, we must understand the meaning of the Arabic word *dīn*, often translated as religion, but which has no real equivalent in French. This word designates the nature of Islam, not a religion, but a system at once political, religious, military, economic, social and legal, as

76

well as a way of life oriented toward the submission of the individual to a divinity (Allah) and his prophet or messenger (Muhammad).[293] In Arabic and in the Koran, Islam means submission, total obedience. *Dīn* means submission and adoration of the Creator, the Master. Islam rules every aspect of existence (spiritual, intellectual, moral and practical); it is total submission toward Allah alone and life in conformity with the teachings of Muhammad.[294]

A journalist with the Pickering Post inquired whether Imam Habib Bewley would be treated as "racist" for having dared to denounce the halal certification racket.[295] According to the Imam, there are two fundamental principles within dīn: firstly, everything is halal per se, and secondly, Allah is the only legislator.

> They should not be asking people to pay extra to declare that their products are halal. By doing so, they do exactly what Allah reproaches Jewish Rabbis with when he says in the al-Baqara Surat: "Do not exchange My revelations for a small price." It is totally reprehensible to profit from certain rules of life of our religion. […] through the pursuit of profit at the cost of common sense and the sale of seals destined for wrapping products such as water, toothpicks, and pepper. This is an entirely abusive use of the system. It is as if Allah's religion were reduced to food—the only thing which distinguishes us from our non-Muslim counterparts is that we put a halal label on our gummy bears. Is this really all our religion consists in, and is this what our entire ulema [body of scholars] should be occupying their time and energy to discuss and argue?[296]

The norms listed by the website of the Halal Montreal Authority[297] well illustrate the problem exposed by Imam Bewley. Their certifications run from simple blueberries (Bleuet Nordic Inc. and Bleuets Mistassini Ltée) to the zinc oxide contained in baby powder! Elsewhere, even some metal conveyer belts are certified halal!

The American company Cambridge Engineered Solutions (CES) manufactures metallic conveyer belts for the food industry; they have been certified halal by Islamic Services of America (ISA) since 2014. Here is an extract from an interview with a CES spokesman:

> A label from an independent certification agency procures for food producers—and, in the end, for consumers—the assurance that nothing haram (forbidden) has been used during preparation, cooking,

refrigeration or wrapping of the food. "For the 1.5 billion Muslims in the world, halal certification indicates that meat, poultry, bakery products and other foodstuffs they eat have been prepared according to Islamic dietary rules," says Tyler. "Unfortunately, most food producers do not realize that the rolling metal carpets of their conveyer belts have traditionally been produced with impermissible animal-based lubricants, sometimes pork fat." The Cambridge company says that it uses 100% synthetic products in manufacturing its conveyer belts. The company voluntarily opted for halal certification to guarantee its commercial customers that its conveyer belts—an integral part of the production process—respect Islamic dietary principles.[298]

An institution called The Message of Islam cites an anecdote. When the faithful asked the prophet whether they could eat from the same plates as Christians or Jews, he answered: "Don't do so unless you cannot find others. In that case, wash them before eating from them."[299] A quick wash, and the matter is resolved. In sum: washing someone else's plate before eating out of it is fairly ordinary, but to go from there to certifying steel…

A Business that Contradicts the Spirit of Islam?

The modern idea of a halal business may be denounced by practicing Muslims for the following reason: The term *bid'ah* (innovation, new idea, heresy) refers to a thing invented on the basis of no preceding model. In the context of Sunni Islam: "innovation refers to a made-up religious path which resembles the Islamic legal path. It is sought by exaggerating this path in the adoration of Allah."[300] Here is a frequently cited sacred text:

> According to Al-'Irbad ibn Sâiya: Allah's messenger gave a sermon which filled our hearts with fear and made our tears flow. We said to him: 'Oh messenger of Allah! This seems like the sermon of someone saying goodbye forever. So give us a few recommendation.' He said: 'I recommend that you fear Allah, listen and obey him even if your emir is a slave. He among you who shall live will see great divergences. Follow my sunna and the sunna of the rightly guided caliphs. Cling to it, chew it with your molars. And be on guard against innovation (in religion), for any innovation is error.[301]

Innovation is opposed to Islam because it implies that this religion is incomplete and imperfect. The introduction of new ideas into Islam is therefore supposed to be forbidden. But few religious authorities seem to make much ado about this, and the halal industry even less. The Edelweiss and Écolait companies wish to create a buzz about their new halal veal ham.[302] New halal tests perfected by the Franco-Algerian company Capital Biotech to detect pork or alcohol in foodstuffs are selling like hotcakes.[303] A meat test to show whether the animal was slaughtered without stunning is about to go on the market!

How much longer will we have to wait for a test to determine whether a person is Christian, Jewish, Atheist, Buddhist, Heretic or Apostate?

CHAPTER THREE

RITUAL SLAUGHTER

A Question of Principle

The question of the kosher and halal ritual slaughter of animals as set out in this chapter does not aim at ostracizing any individual or community in any way. Let us be clear: very few communities are qualified to give lessons on the subject of animal treatment. No one has a monopoly on mistreatment or cruelty, so our indignation on this score should not be selective. This subject, which is rightly controversial, is inseparable from the thorny question of religious certification. In both cases, only a debate centered on the defense of clearly established principles can aspire to any sort of legitimacy. It is not, then, freedom of religion which is at stake, but the ways in which its exercise may infringe on public values. Taking into account the scientific character of the arguments advanced in this book, any imputations of motive or insinuations of anti-Semitism and/or Islamophobia can be seen as a matter of bad faith—or indeed, of defamation—pure and simple.

From Multiculturalism to Legal Pluralism

The pernicious cultural relativism of multicultural policies has allowed religious fundamentalists quietly to impose legal pluralism on the Canadian legal system. This is why the norms for producing kosher and halal meat obey Hebrew and Islamic law respectively, and not the laws of the country.[304] At a time when religious fundamentalism is prominent in the news, it is more pertinent than ever to criticize certain practices which our easygoing, opportunistic and irresponsible states have endorsed both in their legislation and in their economies in defiance of the majority of its citizens' freedom of conscience.

At the beginning, kosher and halal applied mainly to meat, which remains a major source of revenue for certifiers, along with a range of products unknown in the age of the Bible and Koran. This yawning gap allows us to see how few scruples certain fundamentalists and greedy businessmen have about raking in as much as they can.

The movement toward a generalization of kosher and halal, with whole production chains being converted, will continue for as long as it is not stopped: the case of France, with its astronomical percentage of halal slaughter, is proof enough. The existence of this practice should in no way be considered a permanently established right, nor should its religious basis or legal character (affirmed by legal exemptions and "elastic" legal charters) or any sort of industrial logic shield it from criticism.

Whatever party is in power, successive politicians continue to take shelter behind freedom of religion and permissiveness in order to avoid the whole question, and to avoid irritating businessmen, lobbies and possible voters who keep their eye on the ball.

Created in 2007, the Bouchard-Taylor Commission tried to make people believe that reasonable accommodation amounted to respect for "cultural differences" and the integration of immigrants, whereas they are motivated by religion nearly 100% of the time. By disguising religion as culture, the administrators lent legitimacy to the increased intrusion of religion into the public sphere.

The Challenge to Ritual Slaughter Is Based Upon the Defense of Fundamental Values

Any courageous legislative protection of secularism should also deal with religious certification and ritual slaughter. From the Netherlands to Australia by way of Quebec, there is persistent unease over the slaughter of animals without preliminary stunning, prohibited in certain other countries.[305]

We must avoid any ambiguity regarding the finality of the struggle to prohibit these practices and the industry built upon them. Ritual slaughter of animals is contrary to three fundamental values: the separation of state and religion, the universality of the common good, and ethics.

The Three Reasons for the Struggle
Against Ritual Slaughter

1. The secular character of public institutions

A truly secular State which protects the common good and guarantees social cohesion must enact rules based on rational principles that apply to all citizens without exception. The religious exceptions legalizing ritual slaughter violate this concept of equality. In principle, laws are a set of rules applicable to all, established by the sovereign authority of the State, which enact rights, duties and coercion in the name of the common good. Human nature being as it is, they also come from a determination to define and prevent certain abuses.

But the absence of an unequivocal separation of religion from the State undermines the very essence of law. The Preamble to the Charter of Rights and Freedoms enshrined in the Canadian Constitution— "Whereas Canada is founded upon principles that recognize the supremacy of God and the rule of law"—is one of the worst blunders ever committed by our legislators. It was certainly not for nothing that Canada adopted in 1959 a law on humane slaughter. This law states that an animal must not be slaughtered without having been rendered unconscious.

Giving in to pressure from a subsidiary of the Canadian Jewish Council who wanted the technique of slaughtering animals without preliminary stunning (*shehita*) "protected" by law, Prime Minister John G. Diefenbaker in 1960 adopted the *Bill of Rights*, predecessor of our charters of personal rights and freedoms. Preliminary stunning was integrated into the Law on Meat Inspection, which reiterated the exception to stunning if the animal is slaughtered according to a rite conformable to Jewish or Islamic law, or if the animal is killed "by rapid, complete and simultaneous cutting of the jugular and carotid veins so that it loses consciousness immediately" (Article 77). This last point has been invalidated by the international scientific community.

In Quebec, the Minister of Agriculture, Fisheries and Food (MAFFQ) integrated the exception to article 77 into article 6.4.2.2 of his food regulations while avoiding the terms "suffering" and "cruelty" present in the Federal Criminal Code—a way of disregarding impunity all the better to establish it?

In 2012, article 55.9.15 of proposed Law 51 modifying Law P-42 on the Sanitary Protection of Animals stated: "Notwithstanding the provisions of the present section, the ritual practices prescribed by a religion remain permitted." This wording is sufficiently evasive to give carte blanche to any abuse.

Having been taken over by Ottawa, the government of Quebec is abdicating its responsibilities to benefit a system supported by groups whose interest conflict with one another. The law on food products, however, says it can, by means of regulations, "determine the material and installation to be used, the methods to follow and the norms to respect for the treatment of animals while at the slaughterhouse or for the slaughter of animals without cruelty." In Quebec, 34 establishments under federal jurisdiction perform ritual slaughter (an interprovincial and international business). Our attempts to find out from MAFFQ the exact number of those under provincial jurisdiction and precise statistics on ritual slaughter were unsuccessful. It is obvious there is no political will to give a public accounting of industries complicit with religious fundamentalism. By its (hardly disinterested) indulgence of the ritually slaughtered meat industry, the government of Quebec is failing in its duty of neutrality.

2. Granting primacy to common values

The charters protect freedom of belief, and not freedom to act according to particular and arbitrary beliefs. But this is what our indulgent governments are authorizing through the "legal" intrusion of religious norms into the matter of animal slaughter for consumption. Entrusted by MAFFQ with setting up and managing the system for identifying and tracing animals, the company Agri-Traçabilité Québec told us they collect no data on the methods of slaughter used. Meat products from ritually slaughtered animals enter the conventional product circuit in indeterminate number. In an interview, Rabbi Saul Emanuel admitted:

> Of every 100 animals slaughtered, only 27-30 are considered kosher....
> They are not sick. It is only because their lungs are not smooth—glatt—
> that they are marked. That meat goes to the non-kosher market.[306]

One can just imagine the public hue and cry if the slaughter of animals according to the rules of sharia were mentioned on meat labels. "Quebec supermarkets Metro and Sobeys say they have no specific halal department, but acknowledge that a number of their products are always halal."[307] The Quebec company Avicomax which slaughters 200,000 chickens every week channels 40% of its production to the standard non-Muslim market.[308] And what about the unsold products customized for the targeted communities, or the meat served in restaurants, educational institutions, hospitals and prisons?

Not having the relevant information, Canadian citizens who do not belong to the religious communities to which halal or kosher norms apply are deprived of the right to choose or refuse a product according to their personal convictions. They are also kept in ignorance of the effects of certification on the price of grocery items, and of where the money goes. Consequently, these opaque and discriminatory commercial practices[309], accepted by Canada and the provincial governments, constitute a serious violation of the right to equality as regards freedom of conscience[310].

3. Animal protection

Whether connected with freedom of worship or not, any form of abuse of animals is reprehensible. Slaughter without adequate preliminary stunning involves unnecessary suffering: there are abundant scientific proofs to this effect. As soon as practices prove to be a source of unjustifiable suffering, they should be condemned on the same grounds as any other form of mistreatment or abuse of animals.

Slaughter without preliminary stunning is one case among a vast repertoire of abuse affecting an enormous number of animals used for human ends.[311] The fight against ritual slaughter must be guided by questions of principle applicable to all other cases involving animal well-being. Many veterinarians, researchers, biologists or consultants in the food processing sector condemn ritual slaughter for ethical reasons. "Animal well-being should have precedence over religious beliefs," declares Dr. John Blackwell in the name of the British Veterinary Association and its 14,000 members.[312]

There are certainly important reasons behind the law against animal cruelty in the Canadian Criminal Code:

> Article 445.1 (1) Anyone is guilty of an infraction who a) voluntarily causes or, if he is the proprietor, voluntarily allows to be caused any unnecessary pain, suffering or wound to an animal or bird....

85

Our Charters of Personal Rights and Freedoms sets up absolute principles such as "Everyone has fundamental freedoms [...] such as freedom of religion." It is irresponsible not to have added that: "Freedom of worship must not be exercised so as to provide an excuse or authorization for violating rules meant to protect animals." By allowing illegal activity to be made legal, federal and provincial charters and legislation expose many animals to unreasonable practices in the name of freedom of worship. In slaughterhouses under the jurisdiction of Quebec Province, 20% of red meat is from halal slaughter, and thus exempt from the laws against cruelty to animals, as too often are other types of mistreatment of livestock in general.[313] But today's exaggerated ritualism may obscure the original claims of religion. Judaism preaches the avoidance of all cruelty toward animals: the famous principle tza'ar ba'alei chayim ["suffering of living creatures"]. Even Muhammad, the prophet of Islam, is said according to his early biographers to have eaten meat only four times in his life, nourishing himself on vegetables, fruits and honey.

There have been exceptional cases of sincere respect for animals in all human communities. A survivor of the Nazi concentration camp Dachau, Edgar Kupfer-Koberwitz, published his journal, written in secret between 1940 and 1945, in which he explained why he was a vegetarian: "I refuse to eat animals because I cannot nourish myself with the sufferings and death of other creatures. I refuse to act this way because I suffer so much myself and I can feel the sufferings of others." In 1967, the American Rabbi Eugen Kullman took part in a campaign in the New York Times against the slaughter of unstunned animals. The former Grand Rabbi of Ireland David Rosen recommends a meatless diet. Montreal's Orthodox Rabbi Scharchar Orenstein is a vegetarian from ethical, health, and environmental considerations. And Israel has one of the highest per capita rates of vegetarianism in the world.

This type of dissent is rarer in the Muslim world, but several examples can be cited, e.g., the mystical current called "Sufism" born in the 7th Century; the philosopher Al-Ghazali (1050-1111); the anonymous Brethren of Purity (Ikhwan al-Safa) group who implacably polemized against the sufferings of cattle; the Grand Mufti of Marseille Soheib Bencheikh, who has cast doubt in our own days on the need to slaughter sheep for Eid-el-Kabir; and a call for compassion towards animals by a London Imam.[314]

Opposition to the ritual slaughter of animals has absolutely nothing to do with anti-Semitism or Islamophobia. Multiculturalism's strength lies in its success in imposing the idea that an individual and his culture are the same thing. This is what allows the semantic conflation of the words "critic" and "racist," which has left a mess behind it. Just as software does not belong to the core of an operating system, a physical person is not a culture; he "inherits" a culture (which can also contain subcultures), and has two kinds of traits: one of them immutable and acquired at birth or from circumstance, and the other changeable and connected to education. One's ethnic group, the color of one's skin, one's sex, age, physical characteristics, handicaps, sexual orientation are all unchosen statuses of the individual, and their immutability is the reason no discrimination should be practiced against persons on such bases.

Because of their variable and alterable character, customs, traditions, clothing and cooking styles, philosophies, religious rites and beliefs, artistic and intellectual displays can be criticized and form the object of discussion and change. This is a capital point, and reveals the ideological trap of multiculturalism. According to the Larousse dictionary, the word "fundamentalism" is defined as follows: "An attitude and disposition of certain religious persons who, in the name of uncompromising respect for tradition, refuse any change." There is nothing immoral in denouncing ritual slaughter techniques, since these have a reversible character. The rule of preliminary stunning of animals and the law against cruelty to animals in our Criminal Code are examples of ethical principles, just as are laws against economic crimes, child pornography, drug dealing, transportation security, etc. It is not hard to see that these social codes are neither racist nor discriminatory. In 2002, the Canadian Jewish Congress (CJC), in the name of the Jewish and Muslim communities, attempted to have the animal cruelty section of the Criminal Code modified to protect ritual slaughter from all possible challenge in its name. Is this an implicit admission?

Kosher Meat

The first orthodox Jewish immigrants to Canada brought their ancestral religious practices with them. The Shearith Israel Synagogue was built in 1768 when the Jewish community of Montreal amounted to barely 200 people. The first kosher butcher's shop in Montreal opened in 1884. The men who practiced the trade of slaughterer (*shohet*) used a slaughter technique without stunning (*shehita*) that had not changed for centuries. The demand for kosher meat grew in tandem with the increase in the Jewish population. This larger market in turn greatly expanded certification revenues.

In its beginnings, the kosher meat market was a real free-for-all: in his analysis of the condition of the rabbinate in New York in 1896, Gerson Rosenzweig, editor of the magazine The Hebrew, accused Rabbi Drachman of having granted "tens of thousands of attestations." He wrote of Drachman:

> Dr. So-and-so who lives uptown and is a rabbi according to their criteria but not according to ours. Taking the title Head Rabbi, he came to an agreement with the butchers and proclaimed himself Grand Rabbi on the spot.[315]

Rosenzweig states that the *shochetim* and the butchers who did not observe the Sabbath paid rabbis to certify their meat kosher.

At stake was the question of who would control this industry, and Montreal was not to be outdone. Eliezer Segal in his article *Shorter by a Head: Kosher Crime in the Roaring '20s*,[316] describes the merciless war between two rabbis determined not to let such control elude their grasp. For several decades, kosher meat, produced according to the demands of Jewish Law, has received a certification from a rabbi (or rabbinical organization) and bear a corresponding seal.

In Quebec, there is a slaughterhouse for cattle and two for veal, including Écolait in the La Plaine suburb of Montreal, where Rabbis and Muslim slaughterers rub shoulders. There is also an important producer of kosher poultry, Marvid Poultry. The synchronization of kosher and halal slaughter is explained by the fact that they are very similar. Kosher differs from halal in its inspection of animals before and after slaughter according to the precise instructions of Jewish Law (halakha), as well as by the form of the knife and the prayer involved.

Now, as we have already mentioned, the rules of kashruth are followed by a very small percentage of the Jewish community. There are three currents within Judaism: Reform, Conservative and Orthodox. The latter group is the only one which considers the observance of halakha obligatory and unchanging.[317] Ultra-Orthodox Jews see to it that shehita endures. In Montreal, 12% of Jews consider themselves Haredim, and 80% of these are Hassidic Jews.

A Tradition Handed Down from Another Age

What is the historical basis of the tendency to ritual sacrifice among peoples of Abrahamic culture such as Jews and Arabs? Is it simply a survival of a primitive cult tied to the Canaanite divinity Moloch Ba'al practiced all along the Tigris and Euphrates? In the hope of bounteous harvests, the inhabitants sacrificed their firstborn in order to have "the eye of the gods." Later on, children were replaced by animals.[318]

Although the Torah does not give any specific rules for kosher slaughter, Deuteronomy 12: 21—"You may kill any of your herd and flock which the LORD has given you, as I have commanded you"—was interpreted to mean that God transmitted his instructions orally. Rabbis later extrapolated from these supposed "divine rules."

The tractate *Chullin* of the Talmud (2nd-3rd Century AD) describes the technique of ritual slaughter called shehita. The words *shehita* and *shohet* have as their common root the Hebrew word spelled *Shin-Chet-Tav* and meaning "to kill." The avoidance of consuming blood is one of the pillars of kashruth. Given the state of knowledge of the time, *shehita* must have been the best practice in the eyes of those who codified the law. Anchored in superstition (from which any idea of preliminary stunning was absent), it is curious to see carried over to our own day the myth that *shehita* is the most humane way of slaughtering an animal; this is strongly contested by contemporary science. Another myth is that "only *shehita* assures that meat contains no blood," which is not true: animals slaughtered in the conventional fashion have been bled completely before they are processed. Prof. Anil of the University of Bristol and his team have compared slaughter with and without preliminary stunning and measured the volume of blood obtained: they are exactly the same.[319]

It is often said that there is no disputing faith. Still, the practitioners of *shehita* do not hesitate to offer scientific arguments when doubt is cast on their practices. The careful examination of sources cited by the Jewish Lobby are very revealing of a corporate spirit which takes little account of conflicts of interest.

We may note that the practice of *shehita* is forbidden to women, even cutting a chicken's throat, a flagrant violation of the principle of the equality of men and women. This is a case of workplace discrimination which deprives women of access to thousands of jobs.

Shehita for Dummies

1. The slaughterer or one who sacrifices: the shehita is carried out by a practicing Jew called a *shohet* (knowledgeable of the rules of kashruth, although not necessarily a Rabbi). He must be recognized as having the competence to carry out ritual slaughter.

2. The kosher animal: the fully conscious animal to be slaughtered must be in perfect health, i.e., neither sick nor injured nor castrated. For this reason, preliminary insensibilization with a percussion pistol or by electrical stunning are "incompatible" with ritual slaughter. It is demanded that an animal be 100% intact when it is killed in order to be considered kosher, but the severing of the tracheal artery, esophagus, jugular and carotid veins do not present any problem. The *shohet* first carries out a minute inspection of the animal in 18 points. He assures himself that there is no grain of sand or particle on the animal's neck. Depending on the historical period and the Jewish sect involved, the animal may be positioned in several ways, either on the ground, on its back (*shechita munachas*), or standing, with its head inserted in a halter (*shechita meumad*).[320] Birds are suspended by their claws. As with halal, the animals have for centuries been the occasion of semantic ambiguity between the words "alive" and "conscious."

3. The ancient method: the animal was simply overturned on the ground and its throat was cut.

4. *Shechita munachas* (the hoisting method): this method was established in slaughterhouses during the 20th Century for sanitary reasons. The animal is suspended by a hoof and its throat cut. According to Rabbi Menachem Genack of the Orthodox union, this is the preferred method in Israel.

5. *Shechita meumad*—the method of holding upright: also according to Rabbi Genack, this is the method preferred from a halakhic point of view by the Orthodox Union.

6. *Shechita meumad*—method of holding down: pure barbarism, to judge from the few examples circulating on the internet.

7. The Knife (*halef*): the shohet first examines the knife with which he will slaughter the animal. This knife, called a *halef*, usually measures 15.24 cm for chickens and nearly 50 cm for large livestock. The blade, which never ends in a point, is of equal

breadth along its full length. The shohet makes sure the blade is sharp as a razor and without any indentation or imperfection.

8. The fatal incision (*shehita*): just before killing the animal, the *shohet* says a short prayer announcing that he is about to take a life, then rapidly cuts the throat in a single blow, without cutting arteries, which would render the animal "unkosher." Any hesitation or pressure with the blade renders the meat unconformable. The animal is then suspended upside down to allow bleeding, as in conventional slaughter. In short, it dies when it runs out of blood.

9. Post-mortem inspection (*bediqua*): slaughter is followed by an anatomical examination of the animal, and any lesion is scrutinized to determine whether it leaves the animal suitable for consumption or not. Any sign of sickness or preexisting flaw that might have caused the animal's death within a year renders it illicit. The *shohet* looks, e.g., to whether there are lesions or abscesses on the lungs. If so, the animal is rejected. (For birds, the intestines are checked with particular care.) If there is a lesion on the animal's lung, the *shohet* must determine whether it is a perforation or not—if it is, the animal cannot be considered kosher. But Ashkenazim accept it if the lesion can easily be removed. Although the presence of an adhesion does not necessarily make an animal unkosher, some fundamentalist Jewish communities eat only meat coming from animals without adhesions (i.e., glatt kosher).[321]

The Kashruth Council of Canada (COR) informs us that 70% of slaughtered animals are disqualified upon inspection: "Unfortunately, kosher conformity after inspection of the lungs is only about 30 per cent."[322] Rabbi Saul Emanuel, director of the Montreal certification agency MK, told Janice Arnold of Canadian Jewish News that the remaining animals are passed on to other consumers: "Of 100 animals butchered, only 27-30 are considered kosher. [The others] are not sick. It is only because their lungs are not smooth—glatt—that they are marked. That meat goes to the non-kosher market. "[323]

Formerly, declaring a carcass "not kosher" could mean significant losses for the rabbinical agencies, but not in our time. Kosher slaughterhouses are often affiliated with wholesalers who buy the carcasses rejected by the *shochetim*. The meat is destined for the ordinary market, of course.

Kosherization (Treating Meat)

Deveining, i.e., the removal of veins, suet and residual blood, is the final stage in the ritual preparation of meat following bloodletting. This process, known as *treiboring* (in Yiddish) and *nikkur* (in Hebrew), must be completed within 72 hours following slaughter. Kosher establishments sell only the front parts of the animal for religious reasons. The butcher removes the suet, consumption of which is forbidden because "it was burned on the sacrificial altar of the Temple in Jerusalem" (Leviticus 4: 19).

The sciatic nerve and all its ramifications are forbidden. This comes from the wrestling bout between Jacob and the Angel: "Therefore to this day the Israelites do not eat the sinew of the hip which is upon the hollow of the thigh, because he touched the hollow of Jacob's thigh on the sinew of the hip" (Genesis 32: 32). Because it is so difficult to remove this nerve, it was decided to give up eating the hind quarter of all mammals, which passes into the conventional market (note: the sciatic nerve of birds is not removed). Then the meats are "cleaned."[324] They are soaked thirty minutes in clean water then hung to dry. Once they finish dripping, they are covered in coarse salt and placed on an inclined plane for an hour. Then they are rinsed three times to remove the salt. After the final rinse, the meat is dried, cut in pieces, and wrapped for sale.

In the end, nearly 70 to 90% of meat slaughter *shechita-style* goes into the conventional market without consumers knowing, since labels to do not mention the method of slaughter. In fact, the organization Agri-Traçabilité Quebec, charged by the MAFFQ with managing the database containing the history of each animal slaughtered on its territory, does not record the method of slaughter employed. Hence the impossibility of getting exact statistical information on ritual slaughter in Quebec. There is no transparency, and no political will to change matters.

Glatt Kosher: A Big Step Toward the Fundamentalist Right Dominating Industry

In the 1970s in the United States, Orthodox Jewish Authorities adopted the new ultra-strict standard called "glatt kosher," the only standard acceptable in their eyes. "Regular" kosher was thenceforth relegated to conservative Jews and all those who do not take the rules of kashruth as seriously as they do.[325] Sephardi and Hassidic Jews reject meat from animals whose lungs are not smooth (non-glatt). Glatt kosher meat comes from animals whose post mortem lung examination has revealed absolutely no marks. Nearly all kosher meat sold today is glatt kosher, because it is easier for the shohet not to agonize over such decisions, especially as the rejected carcasses are automatically bought by wholesalers. The kosher caterers at Montreal-Trudeau and Pearson Airports, supervised by Montreal's MK Agency, serve only glatt meat.

But Masorti Jews have taken a dim view of glatt kosher:

> Those who wish to cling to ancient rules and adopt a restrictive stance should be respected, but they should not force their rigid norms on all, or intimidate those with another point of view. For such is the terrible mechanism of escalation. As soon as one clan imposes a more rigid form of discipline, it imposes on others, discrediting them. This is exactly what happened with glatt kosher which disqualified the ordinary kosher norm for meat, or for fruits and vegetables henceforth judged forbidden because of the micro-organisms they might carry. People who eat kosher have learned the hard way that their meat, fruits and vegetables are no longer acceptable for the truly observant. What is called progress can in another sense hide a step backward.[326]

According to Prof. Steven Lapidus, a number of Hassidic Jews in Quebec buy meat prepared by their own community's shohet or approved by their leaders. This automatically excludes the personnel of the great MK and COR certification companies. And the reasons appear to have little to do with religion: "Obviously, such choices have economic ramifications which, in many cases, are perhaps more important than halakhic factors. Rabbinical salaries are a significant element of the kosher supervision business. As one of the few regular sources of revenue within the Jewish economy, kosher slaughter has often aroused—like many other economic conflicts—controversy, acrimony and corruption."[327] One witness even reports that American certifiers are operating in Quebec.

Attempts to Ban Shehita in Israel

Israeli politicians have several times tried to forbid Jewish ritual slaughter. For example, the proposed Prevention of Cruelty to Animals Act

(Protection of animals. Amendment stunning before slaughter), containing the following clauses:

a.) Animals must not be slaughtered before having been stunned, so as to reduce their suffering during slaughter;

b.) The Minister of Agriculture will specify the method of stunning to be used.

A similar bill was proposed in 2000 during the 15th meeting of the Knesset. Former Knesset Member Avraham Poraz of the Shinui Party declared at that time that "the purpose of this proposal is to prevent unnecessary suffering to animals caused by the traditional method of slaughter. The slaughtering of animals will be prohibited unless they have previously been stunned by electric shock preventing suffering." By way of reaction to the most recent proposal of this sort by another member of Shinui during the 16th Session of the Knesset, the Grand Rabbi of Israel Shlomo Amar stated his opposition to the bill, arguing that stunning before slaughter is forbidden by Jewish Law (halakha).[328] However, one of the fundamental weakness of the traditional kosher and halal methods unquestionably remains keeping the spinal cord intact during slaughter. This is the channel responsible for the perception of pain. It is why animals suffer so much from their wounds. Dr. Bruno Fiszon, Rabbi of Metz and Moselle, once defended this practice in these terms: "The shohet must take care to stop at the cervical vertebrae without touching them for fear of damaging the knife".[329] What more is there to say? Seeing is believing; cf. the excellent documentary film *Earthlings* by Shaun Monson.

Halal Meat

In Canada, the production and sale of halal meat (i.e., meat allowed under Islamic Law) is a direct corollary of Muslim immigration during the post-Khomeini era. Despite the absence of any universal consensus on the exact norms to be applied, an industry exempt from the obligation of preliminary stunning—long accorded to Jewish ritual slaughter—was born. In both cases, the animals die when they run out of blood. Despite the supposed tensions between the Jewish and Muslim communities, they are agreed when it comes to defending their respective certifications. They often operate in the same slaughterhouses.[330] Some Muslims even buy their meat from kosher butcher's shops. According to a Quebec study[331], certain distributors of halal meat belong to Jewish companies which even export

94

to Saudi Arabia[332]. The Koranic verse according to which any meat produced by People of the Book (Jews and Christians) was halal was long followed. But modern international competition favors processes able to please even the most hardened Islamic fundamentalists.[333] This tendency is also observed in the new norm "mehadrin kosher" observed by the catering services at Trudeau and Pearson Airports, recognized even by Israeli Hassidim.[334]

Religion in the Arsenal of Marketing Arguments

In the beginning there was a short verse in the Koran, based on the realities of 7th Century life: "Prohibited for you are carrion, blood, the flesh of swine, and animals dedicated to other than God; also the flesh of animals strangled, killed violently, killed by a fall, gored to death, mangled by wild animals—except what you rescue, and animals sacrificed on altars; and the practice of drawing lots. For it is immoral. Today, those who disbelieve have despaired of your religion, so do not fear them, but fear Me."[335]

21st Century livestock are subject to extrapolations from this simple ancient text. Nothing says that the animal must be slaughtered fully "conscious." However, *dhabiha* is the ritual method of slaughter prescribed by Islamic Law (sharia). The word is often erroneously used as a synonym for halal. The expression *dhabiha halal* refers to any piece of meat permitted by Islamic Law.[336] There are passages in the hadiths referring to animals.[337]

Dating to 200 years after the death of Muhammad, the hadiths are collections (reliable or otherwise) of words transmitted orally by faithful Muslims going back to the time of someone who knew the prophet and his associates. They narrate what they remember having heard said or seen done in a given circumstance. There are over 700,000 of these second-hand reports! Many are suspect; their credibility is in proportion to the prestige of those reporting them. These different collections feed the Shiite-Sunni opposition in particular.

Along with the precepts of the Koran, the hadiths form the sunna, whence the name Sunnite for the orthodox current.[338] But the recurring source for ritual slaughter (*Al Mu'amalat*) is in the handbook of Islamic Law *Umdat al-Salik*, written in the 14th Century by Ahmad Ibn Naqib Al-Misri.

95

The Animal Victims of Sharia

The integration of the halal meat market into our economies amounts to swallowing section J17.5 of Sharia Law. Recommended in the process of slaughter are:

1. Turning the animal in the direction of Mecca (the qibla);
2. Sharpening the knife;
3. Rapid cutting (as rapid as possible, without more than two slices);
4. Pronouncing the name of Allah (to summon spiritual grace, by saying Bismillah, as in the sunna. This is obligatory according to the Hanafite School);
5. To bless the prophet (may Allah grant him peace);
6. To cut the larger veins on either side of the neck.[339]

The Quebec Ministers of Agriculture and their assistants repeat that halal slaughter is legal by virtue of the Charter of Personal Rights and Freedoms and the Law on food products, statements which clash with those of the Danish Minister of Agriculture Dan Jorgensen, who made preliminary stunning obligatory beginning February 17, 2014. The Jewish and Muslim communities of Denmark have both openly criticized this decision, invoking the fact that it tramples on their religious rights, but Minister Jorgensen has responded that "animal rights have priority over religious rights."[340] It is not surprising that the Quebec Muslim Association has made the following revealing recommendation before the Bouchard-Taylor Commission in 2007: "To preserve the Charter of Personal Rights and Freedoms as it stands without any hierarchy between the different rights and freedoms."[341]

Conventional Slaughter vs. Halal Slaughter

In 1959, Canada adopted the Law on animal slaughter without cruelty, stating that an animal must not be slaughtered before having been rendered unconscious. This decision was integrated into the Law on the inspection of meats, which reiterated the exemption from stunning if the animal is "slaughtered according to a rite conformable to Jewish or Islamic Law," or if the animal is killed "by the rapid, complete and simultaneous slicing of the jugular and carotid arteries so that it loses consciousness immediately" (Article 77).

The two most frequently employed forms of stunning are:

1. Percussion: the percussion pistol is activated by a trigger and causes a concussion at the point of impact. Using compressed air or a blank cartridge, the shock is powerful enough that the animal loses consciousness.

2. Electronarcosis: a procedure of stunning by electrical shock used with calves, sheep and poultry.

The data which follow come from Vigilance halal:

The conventional way of slaughtering cattle: after stunning, the animal (whose heart is still beating) is suspended head down and a longitudinal (not transversal) incision is made in the sternum to cut the blood vessels without touching the trachea and esophagus which is immediately tied to prevent any contamination. This is possible because the stunned animal does not move. One knife is used for the skin and a second for the internal structures.

"Halal" slaughter is quite different. Because the trachea, esophagus and principle veins and arteries of the neck are cut without stunning, and the vertebral column is still intact, the animal does not lose consciousness immediately. The brain continues to receive blood from the two vertebral arteries; clotting on the sliced arteries and veins, which is very common, slows down bleeding; since the trachea is next to the esophagus, there can be cases of regurgitation with inhalation to the lungs, a significant health risk.[342]

According to what some people say, there is no disputing religious beliefs. This would be true if the practitioners of halal abstained from using scientific arguments to justify ritual slaughter, but that is far from being the case.[343] Invariably cited in all pro-halal propaganda are the experiments carries out in 1974-78 by Professor of Veterinary Medicine Wilhelm Schultze (assisted by Prof. Hazim) at the University of Hannover in Germany (a comparative study with electrodes on animals slaughtered with and without stunning). Schulze, however, later cast doubt on the validity of his own experiment due to defective stunning equipment.[344] But Muslims continue to cite it as proof of the superiority of dhabiha at sparing animals suffering.[345]

In March 2002, Canadian deputy-veterinarian André Simard justifiably expressed unease regarding animal suffering, sanitary risks and the absence of transparence associated with *dhabiha*.[346] Relayed by the mass media, the responses of authorities seeking to calm public opinion ignored certain basic scientific principles as well as constraints associated with the great speed of industrial slaughterhouses and the absence of permanent inspectors in several Quebec slaughterhouses styled "local" (or "transitory"). Hélène Trépanier, a veterinarian with the QMAFF, explains that "the standard method of ritual slaughter consists in cutting the blood vessels of the animal's neck rapidly. It is the lack of blood to the brain which brings about the loss of consciousness. Normally in our slaughterhouses the animal will lose consciousness rapidly, and if that is not the case, very quickly the inspection personnel will ensure that the animal is stunned so that this does not continue," she explains. Moreover, in ritual slaughter as in conventional slaughter, the esophagus is tied to keep the contents of the stomach from leaving and avoiding any risk of contamination. Joël Bergeron, Veterinary Doctor and President of the Order of Veterinary Doctors of Quebec, believes that "when the technique is well-applied, there is no risk of contamination."[347]

But how can there be constant surveillance of possible signs of suffering and the systematic tying of all animals' esophagus when there are not permanent inspectors or veterinarians everywhere? This fault is confirmed by Dr. Thérèse Loubier, veterinarian and coordinator of meat inspection for QMAFF, when she was called upon to comment on the illegal slaughter of lambs for Eid el-Kebir:

Ritual slaughter is permitted and regulated. The person who carries it out must demonstrate that he has the dexterity necessary to assure rapid bleeding so that the animal loses consciousness quickly. If experience shows this is not the case, a stunner should be used immediately in order to end the animals suffering. The professional agrees that in small slaughterhouses which do not have a permanent inspector from the Ministry, nothing guarantees that this is done.[348]

The alarm sounded by veterinarian André Simard does not seem to have shaken up the industry. La Presse reported the response of the president of the halal slaughterhouse Louis Lafrance and Son, now under Nigerian ownership:

"There can be no question of changing anything about this technique which roused a certain controversy last Spring." "Customer satisfaction is more important than the word halal," says Indira Moudi, the company's CEO.[349]

Muslim Disagreement about Stunning Before Slaughter

An astronomical number of disturbing videos[350] on the internet have instilled in public opinion a very negative image of halal slaughter. Some Muslim organizations[351], claiming to "care about animal well-being," have tried to improve that image by accepting the stunning of cattle, sheep or birds via reversible methods such as electronarcosis and the percussion pistol. But what is not being said is that such stunning equipment is operated at very low intensity. Low frequency electronarcosis (less than 100 Hz) is used to facilitate the slaughter of the animal by the butcher and to avoid damaging the animals' tissue and organs, not to reduce its sensibility. (A combination of high frequency and low intensity can immobilize a bird, but not render it insensible.)

Although the stunning practiced before conventional slaughter sometimes fails because of unscrupulous butchers or the rapid pace of work, the restrictive norms of JAKIM[352], the largest halal certifier in the world, based in Malaysia, are hardly reassuring from the animals' point of view:

The air pressure in the pistol must not exceed $225kg/cm^3$ and must be gauged at the strict minimum necessary to stun the animal. The blood flow from the halal cut must initially be accompanied by an arterial pulse indicating that the animal is still alive at the moment of halal slaughter. During bloodletting, the cardiac functions must be maintained for at least 60 seconds.

Halal and Kosher both want an "intact" animal, without objecting to consuming the meat of an animal whose trachea and esophagus have been unceremoniously butchered. In a university study[353] we learn that some Montreal artisanal butchers and Imams do not agree with the preliminary stunning accepted by the Islamic Society of North America (ISNA). Is this connected with the rise of radical Islam on the territory of Quebec?

Meanwhile, in the Kingdom of Quebekistan...

In Quebekistan, 18 of the 36 federal slaughterhouses practice halal slaughter. About 15% of cattle and 32% of calves are slaughtered halal-style in the federal slaughterhouses of Canada.[354] Of the 23 slaughterhouses under Quebec's jurisdiction, 6 practice ritual slaughter. This practice is also observed in 11 of the 61 slaughterhouses called "transitory."[355] It also appears that small privately-owned farms make use of clandestine slaughterhouses.

Quebekistan by itself appears to furnish 80% of the veal consumed in Saudi Arabia.[356] Unfortunate byproducts of Quebec's milk industry, more than 500,000 claves born each year have a good chance of suffering a cruel death.

The South African Imam Habib Bewley[357] and the sheiks belonging to the Islamic missionary society "The Message of Islam" based in Riyadh, Saudi Arabia, can contradict contemporary halal orthodoxy all they want, Quebekistan seems determined to keep its status as a "distinct kingdom" on the model of Canadistan. Fatwas stipulate that one must distinguish between *ad-dhakah*, i.e., the sacrifice of meat intended for consumption (which is not an act of worship) and sacrifice intended to approach Allah (which is an act of worship). "Regarding the sacrifice of meat intended for consumption, it is not worship, so there is no reason to recommend facing in the direction of the Qibla (Mecca)."[358] And "no text allows one to specify that slaughter must be carried out by hand."[359]

According to some Muslim authorities, pronouncing the name of Allah or any other God is not even necessary. But in Quebekistan, "sharia sells"[360], and the majority of parties involved in this market say they proceed as follows with the animal:

1. The animal must be "alive" (a word confounded with "conscious");
2. The animal must be turned to face Mecca and an "authorized" Muslim must say Bismillah Rahim wa Allah Akbar ("In the name of God, God is great") just before carrying out the slaughter;
3. The trachea and esophagus must be sliced through without touching the vertebral column (so that the spinal column remains intact).

On the website of Viandes Giroux we read: "A certifier from the East Angus factory in Estrie ensures that the stages of slaughter respect sharia law."[361] The Louis Lafrance slaughterhouse, a major player in halal slaughter in Quebekistan, has created a stir: "But more important than anything else, to obtain halal certification, the task of cutting the animal's throat must be carried out by a Muslim who sees to it that the beast is facing East, in the direction of Mecca, before completing the task."[362] The chicken slaughtered by Avicomax[363] and Giannone[364] is blessed and bled by hand facing East. An Imam comes to bless the animals at the beginning of the first and second work shifts at the Olymel factory in Saint-Damase.[365]

100

El Rancho's halal quail, reports a journalist from La Presse, are blessed by a Muslim butcher: "Here I must say a Muslim prayer to the effect that I am there to slaughter the quails." Does this halal procedure disturb Mr. Andrade, the CEO of the company, who is not a Muslim? "On the contrary, it suits me fine," he says; "it gives my employees work and keeps the economy rolling."[366]

In a corporate video[367], the Director of Montreal Halal Certification, Taibi Baaja, states "that halal meats are hygienic and 'better for health,' that they are good for non-Muslims." More hygienic? There are, however, occasional recalls of halal meat, whether because they were not prepared so as to insure their harmlessness (Viandes Nada import-export[368]), or because of possible E. coli contamination (Maple Lodge Farms[369]). Délices Al-Manar also plays the "health" card on its website.[370] So does the Ontario company Halal Choice.[371] But according to the international norms of the Codex Alimentarius, article 4.2, it is forbidden to say that "halal is better for health": "In conformity with the revised text of the General Directives of the Codex on allegations, the halal seal must not be used so as to cast doubt on the safeness of such food or to give the impression that halal foods have superior nutritional value or are better for health than other foods."[372]

Belly Before Thought

According to a report by the journalist Sarah Bélisle, many purchasers of halal meat are non-Muslims.[373] Encouraging the market in halal meat is a way of supporting implantation of the rules of the *Al-Mu'amalat* (the section of sharia relating to human activities).

Those of our compatriots who believe their stomach is more important than the threat of radical Islam should consider what follows. The famous Al-Azhar University in Egypt famously used to teach its students cannibalism.[374] In the regions of the world where jihadists and sharia dominate, knife blades pass indifferently from human to animal necks. In Syria there have been immolations of Christians, i.e., genuine "human slaughterhouses."[375] On February 15, 2015 the newspaper USA Today carried a Reuters/Associated Press dispatch to the effect that 21 Egyptian Christians in Libya were decapitated by the Islamic State, who issued a video of this butchery.[376] If nothing is done to halt the spread of the area where sharia is applied, the complacency and opportunism of our political leaders and their court businessmen will quite simply hand our civilization over to the slaughterhouse.

Justifiable Controversies

The question of ritual slaughter (in their strictest application) where in every case the animal must die exclusively from blood loss, is causing unease in several Western countries. But the criteria of critical analysis in regard to this issue should apply equally to any other form of morally blameworthy treatment or use of animals. The respect due to animals does not begin at their death, but at their birth. Kosher and halal slaughter of animals without stunning is a universal philosophical and moral matter by the same title as industrial scale livestock farming, calf hutches, fattening of geese, bear bile farming, puppy mills, bullfighting, whale hunting, sport hunting,[377] experimentation with lab animals, etc. All the more so in that the shechita and dhabiha lobbies use supposedly scientific arguments to defend their practices—their commercial practices, that is. Since these do not stem exclusively from religious and supernatural beliefs, it is legitimate to include them in the vast domain of questions connected with the well-being and status of animals, as well as questioning certain dietary dogmas.

Consequently, describing any questioning of ritual slaughter as "racist" amounts to defamation. Moreover, this is a slanderous muddying of the waters, since racism aims at a particular people. What national or racial group is targeted by criticism of these controversial practices? None.

No Smoke Without Fire

As Rabi Yair Hoffman observes, the Jewish method of slaughter (*shehita*) is at the center of a struggle that has been going on nearly two centuries. The field of battle includes Europe, Australia, England, the United States, Israel and South America. It involves militant animal rights activists against rabbis, moderate activists against radicals, and rabbis against rabbis.[378]

Beginning in 1855, the British Society for the Protection of Animals (RSPCA) demanded the prohibition of Jewish ritual slaughter because of the unreasonable suffering associated with it. In 1893, Switzerland banned *shechita* following a popular referendum. The Farm Animal Welfare Council, which has made the same demand since 1895 (later adding halal

102

slaughter) went back on the attack in 2003.[379] But the British government does not listen to the experts. The online petition demanding obligatory stunning for all animals launched in 2015 by the British Veterinary Association (BVA), representing 14,000 members, collected over 100,000 signatures[380] with the help of the RSPCA, which amounts to a clear message. The President of the BVA, Dr. John Blackwell, made clear that the veterinarians' opposition was concerned with animal well-being and had nothing to do with religion ("Animal rights should come before religious beliefs"[381]). The fight continues.

A Canadian Case Which Should Have Set a Legal Precedent

In 1913, Rabbi Abraham Gershom Levitt of Halifax was declared guilty of cruelty to animals in carrying out his functions of *shohet* (kosher slaughterer). Prosecuting him in the name of the Society for the Protection of Animals, Andrew Williamson and the veterinary surgeon Philip Gough testified at the trial. Williamson related that "they had seen an animal attached and suspended head back and muscle and throat exposed, horns touching the ground. The defendant approached and cut the heifer's throat. The animal struggled, struck the ground, kicked with its forelegs and gasped, its tongue sticking out, its throat gargling, all for five minutes; then it was briefly inert and went back to doing the same thing. Fourteen minutes went by between the moment the throat was cut and complete immobility. In my estimation, this involves pain. I lodged a complaint: slaughter involving suffering."

Dr. Gough confirmed that the animal's suffering continued for 12-15 minutes following its throat being cut. Slaughterhouse owners testified, swearing that they rendered animals instantaneously unconscious before slaughter. One of them said Rabbi Levitt systematically refused to take this measure, and another said "the Jewish method was the longest and most painful."[382] More than a hundred years later, in Quebec, the owner of the Abattoir Lawrence wrote on his website: "Slaughter is instantaneous. How anyone could believe that cruelty is an intrinsic part of slaughter (carried out according to the rules) is beyond me. There are other methods of slaughter, such as kosher and halal, which involve bleeding the animal to death without stunning or killing. This is excessively cruel. But the standard practice in North America is the above described. All cerebral activity ceases within a fraction of a second."[383]

The judgment handed down April 23, 1913, by Halifax Judge George H. Fielding was remarkably prescient:

> I look at it this way... I quite understand the view that persons must be cruel in a relative way to kill animals for food, and must take life to get food. If there are two methods by which that can be accomplished and one is more humane than the other, I think the more humane method should be followed. If the least humane method is followed it is unnecessary cruelty. It has been suggested that to convict would deprive a certain portion of the community of food. That may be. I don't see that it is necessary to slaughter animals in this fashion because pain and suffering is caused which is unnecessary. I cannot see why there should not be a conviction. I have nothing to do but administer the law. To my mind this is a very painful way of killing animals. This method has been practiced for over 3000 years without obstruction, and while perhaps it seems a cruel thing to continue in this way all these many years, still at the same time these people have conscientious scruples and this is the first time the method has been attacked. It is really setting a principle.[384]

Alas, calling on the support of the Montreal Jewish community, Rabi Levitt lodged an appeal and, following another trial, another judge reversed the sentence. Veterinarian Gough's remark remains valid today: "After the cutting of the throat, I would say there was still blood circulating to the brain." McFatridge, one of his veterinary colleagues, came to contradict him for the defense, alleging that "the animal feels no pain during cutting and that the convulsions and kicking are no more than motor reflexes."[385]

A few years later, Norway, Sweden and Iceland mandated stunning before slaughter.

Both Kosher and Halal Methods Become Targets

Muslim ritual slaughter (*dhabiha halal*) is now contested for the same reasons as *Jewish shehita*. Germany had forbidden them, but in 2002 the constitutional Court reversed a decision and imposed an exception in the name of freedom of religion. The European Parliament has several times demanded the banning of slaughter without preliminary stunning.

In 2004 there were shock waves in the United States: the organization People for the Ethical Treatment of Animals (PETA) published a video made in Postville, Iowa, revealing numerous acts of cruelty in the process of kosher slaughter.[386]

On September 1, 2008, the law on the protection of animals which maintains the prohibition against ritual slaughter in Switzerland went into force (although ritual slaughter of birds is still allowed). Let us recall that in 2002 the Swiss Institute of Comparative Law published a legal opinion formally establishing that "Neither the Bible nor the Talmud, nor the Koran, nor the sunna of Muhammad, the two sources of law for Jews and Muslims respectively, contain rules prescribing slaughter without preliminary stunning, nor forbid the consumption of meat from animals which were stunned before bloodletting.[387]

In 2011, at a congress of the Quebec Order of Veterinarians, discordant voices were raised. Professor of Judaic Studies Ira Robinson of Concordia University opined that "kosher slaughter should not be tolerated in the name of freedom of worship." Prof. Martine Lachance, specialist in animal rights at the University of Montreal, affirmed that this method is crueler than conventional slaughter. And it was learned that the Orthodox Jewish Rabbi Schachar Orenstein is a vegetarian for ethical, environmental and health reasons![388]

In March 2012, Quebec Veterinarian André Simard expressed concern about the rise in ritual slaughter in the province: "This is a debate concerning norms, transparency and consumer information." Simard also raised the animal welfare issue. In principle, "all animals should be slaughtered in an unconscious state before the bloodletting which kills it," explained the deputy. "But it is well-known that in religious ritual slaughter the basic prescription is that the animal must be conscious as it is bleed," added the trained veterinarian. "This is very painful," he says. His questioning aims at obtaining "objective, technical and scientific" information.[389] Commenting on the announcement by the then-Minister of Agriculture François Gendron of imminent "tightening" of standards in Quebec's meat industry, Mohamed Ghalem, spokesman for the Halal Meat Association, declared that he did not see the necessity for this: "Norms for animal well-being have already been established for 1500 years. I think this is a misunderstanding connected with Islamophobia."[390]

Also in 2012, on the initiative of the Animal Party, legislators in the Netherlands approved a bill banning ritual slaughter by a vote of 116-30. But intensive lobbying by tiny, highly organized (mostly Jewish) groups charging anti-Semitism (sic) succeeded in convincing the Senate to reject the law in exchange for a compromise, viz., the acceptance of stunning if the slaughtered animal is "not insensitive to pain" within 40 seconds after

105

slaughter. This agreement was later unanimously rejected by the Rabbinical Tribunal of Amsterdam, which also decided not to issue any kosher certification in such cases!

We learn that in France, the period before relieving the animal of intense suffering is even longer: "within 90 seconds." The Dutch position alarmed French Jewish authorities:

According to the Grand Rabbi Bruno Fiszon, who handles such matter for the Central Consistory of France, 45 seconds at a minimum are necessary before stunning [after the throat has been cut]. An argument which notably allowed French public authorities to show their "broadmindedness" in establishing a 90 laps before stunning [and after the throat is cut] in its decree of December 2011 governing ritual slaughter. The danger is that under pressure from animal defenders, France will end up adopting the Dutch solution and cutting the period in half.[391]

Oh dear, those horrible defenders of animals! And as French senator Sylvie Goy-Chavent would discover in the summer of 2013, woe to those who dare to advocate transparency for consumers! She had to file a complaint to police over serious death threats she received (a call "to slash her neck to see how long she would stay conscious") after she recommended, in her capacity as senatorial rapporteur on the meat industry, that producers of meat originating from animals that were not stunned before slaughter be legally required to apply "special labeling".[392] The usual protests by religious spokesmen resonated and since Goy-Chavent's proposal wasn't backed by any politician, it fell into oblivion.

As for What Enlightened Science Says...

Signed by 90 scientists, the letter against ritual slaughter addressed in 2012 to the Polish government, composed by Dr. Antoni Amirowicz of the Institute for the Protection of Nature of the Polish Academy of Sciences and Prof. Jerzy Bańbura of the Dept. of Experimental Zoology and Evolutionary Biology at the University of Lodz is among the most sensible: "Our position rests exclusively on scientific knowledge and moral opposition toward extreme forms of cruelty towards animals, and not on aversion toward religious rituals and practices."[393] Their government listened to them and went ahead: ritual slaughter was banned for nearly two years. But in March 2014, Poland had to resign itself to allowing it once again when the Constitutional Court decided that the prohibition was not conformable to the fundamental law affirming freedom of religion (the Polish Jewish Community had appealed to the Court at the end of August). "Constitutional protection extends to religious activities far from the predominant behavior in a given state, even to those unpopular with most of the society," declared Judge Maria Gintowt-Jankowicz in announcing the decision.[394]

It is rather democracy which is persecuted and in strong need of protection: such exceptions are not supported anywhere in the West if made the subject of popular referenda. Other states have on occasion weathered the storm: since February 2014, ritual slaughter has been banned in Denmark. The Jewish and Muslim communities of the country have openly criticized this decision, invoking the fact it tramples on their religious rights, but Minister Dan Jorgensen responded that "animal rights take priority over religious rights."[395]

Bnai B'rith and ADL Propaganda Passed on by the Media

"Jewish ritual slaughter is often criticized, not to say condemned, by well-intentioned but very badly informed persons," declares Grand Rabbi Michel Gugenheim.

Historical research into the earliest legislation relating to the problem of ritual slaughter reveals that the Jewish religious position has always been the same everywhere. It consists in affirming that scientific studies prove that ritual slaughter causes no suffering to animals. The ADL document distributed by Bnai B'rith, "Jewish Ritual Slaughter, or Respect for the Animal," the preface of which is signed by Rabbi Michel Gugenheim, offers some frequently recurring arguments which seek to counter any possible wish to change the status quo:

> We wish for a very wide diffusion of this document in the hope that it will convince every honest observer of the optimal and exemplary character of this method of slaughter, and that it will win over all those sincerely attached to respect for and the protection of animals.[396] Shechita is founded on an unchanging principle of the Torah: respect for animal life. It involves the need to limit as much as possible the suffering of the animal in the course of slaughter, and does not banalize its death. [...] Any preliminary stunning or anesthesia (electric or chemical) is forbidden, and renders the animal nevela—unsuited to consumption. [...] Measures carried out by numerous professors of animal physiology from different

countries all arrive at the conclusion that there are no signs of suffering in the course of shechita because of the nearly immediately loss of consciousness. [...] All controversy as to the violence of the bloodletting or the reflexive movements of the animal which can occur during shechita is without a scientific basis. [...] The killing of the animal can only be done through shechita, precisely codified on the basis of the fundamental notion of respect for the animal and the need to limit its suffering. [...] Shechita is much superior to bloodletting with preliminary stunning, and promotes healthier meat. These hygienic aspects resulting from shechita must be considered merely as a supplementary advantage, the essential point being to reduce the suffering of the animal.[397]

The text by Bruno Fiszon, Grand Rabbi of Metz and the Moselle, Jewish Dietary Laws: Kashruth, is very similar:

Among its rules of behavior regarding animals, Judaism preaches the exclusion of all cruelty. [...] There exists an elevated form of compassion for animals and a consideration of their suffering in Judaism. Numerous laws, known by the Hebrew term Tza'ar Ba'alei Chayim, forbid such suffering. [...] Ritual slaughter (shechita) allows significant bloodletting. [...] The animal must be conscious, which excludes any preliminary stunning. A contemporary authority, Rav Yitzhak Weiss in his work Minhat Ytzhak, indicates that any anesthesia before slaughter would render the animal unfit for consumption. [...] The shochet must make sure to stop at the vertebral column without touching it for fear of damaging the knife (sic). [...] An object of numerous studies and especially of numerous debates, ritual slaughter is a painless method in comparison to others. To demonstrate this experimentally is beyond the scope of this essay and would require lengthy development. Let us simply specify that the cutting of the carotid artery leads to massive hemorrhaging, which causes a drop in arterial blood pressure in the central nervous system and rapidly puts the neurons out of action (expressed by a loss of consciousness) [...] Man must act to avoid any form of cruelty. It appears that shechita or ritual slaughter practiced according to all the rules of art guarantees limiting animal suffering.[398]

Commenting on the polemic surrounding kosher ritual slaughter in Quebec, Rabbi Saul Emanuel responds that the Torah forbids all cruelty toward animals, and that: "the knife blade used for slaughter must not have the slightest imperfection... It must cut like a razor," he says. "And one must cut quickly with a single blow so that the animal dies instantly." "I have visited numerous slaughterhouses, I have seen conventional and halal slaughter as well as our own, and they are all equally humane."[399]

Recurring Pro-Dhabiha Halal Discourse

The Ontario company Maple Lodge Farms, often criticized in the media for serious cases of cruelty to animals[400], explains the halal process behind its Zabiha Halal products. Among other things, it states that the slaughter instrument must be very sharp so as not to cause unnecessary suffering to the animals. The blood must be correctly drained. At the moment of slaughter, an extremely precise rotary blade slices the respiratory channel, the esophagus, the jugular vein and arteries while leaving the head attached. The spinal column is left intact and the nervous system remains whole in order to assure complete bloodletting.[401]

At the Avicomax slaughterhouse in Drummondville, "a prayer is recited during the slaughter of the chicken which is bled by hand in order to drain it completely."[402] The owner of the halal Châteauguay Butcher Shop, Radouande Ben Rahmanie said in an interview with the newspaper Le Soleil de Châteauguay:

> Even if halal meat rests upon a religious tradition, the butcher tries not to mix religion into his explanations when speaking to clients. There are many other reasons to choose halal meat, he explains. First of all, there is a health aspect, for the halal slaughter technique requires cutting a vein of the animal's neck in order to drain the blood. Blood is considered a disease vector in the Muslim religion.[403]

The Islamic Society of North America (Canada) describes *dhabiha halal* as follows:

> A sharp blade and deftness are required in order to minimize the pain and unnecessary suffering of the animal. This involves rapid slicing of the veins and arteries of the animal's neck, without affecting the spinal cord or nervous system. The massive loss of blood renders the animal unconscious within a few seconds. Leaving the spinal cord intact allows convulsions resulting from the muscular contraction in response to the lack of oxygenation of the cells of the neck. The whole process favors maximal bloodletting, partly eliminating waste material and micro-organisms, thus improving the flavor, shelf-life, and healthfulness of the meat.[404]

109

Regarding halal meat, the Délice Al-Manar company says the following:

> Most animal illnesses transmitted to man are related to the animal's blood, so it is essential to drain the animal's blood in order to minimize all risk of transmission. [...] Some defenders of animal rights prefer it because they believe this method of slaughter is less stressful and causes less suffering (*sic*) to the animal than the method used in conventional slaughterhouses.[405]

But blood is entirely drained during conventional slaughter with preliminary insensibilization!

The authors of *Les enjeux de la viande halal au Québec*[406] ["The Stakes of Halal Meat in Quebec"] cite two sources of arguments of a scientific nature invariably cited by defenders of halal, Wilhelm Schulze[407] and Dr. Jawad Hidmi[408]:

One of the first veterinary studies of Jewish ritual appeared in 1978 in Germany. Its author, W. Schulze, concluded that the religious method of slaughter caused less suffering to the animals: if the jugular veins were sliced completely and rapidly, slaughter causes immediate unconsciousness and is equivalent to stunning (with club, electrocution, toxic gas or scalding in the case of birds). These arguments have long been advanced and are still advanced by Muslim authorities.[409]

The experiment carried out at the University of Hannover in Germany (1974-78) by Professor of Veterinary Medicine Wilhelm Schulze, *"Attempts to Objectify Pain and Consciousness in Conventional (captive bolt pistol stunning) and Ritual (knife) Methods of Slaughtering Sheep and Calves"*[410] is also cited by defenders of kashruth. Schulze however later questioned the validity of his experiment because of defective insensibilization equipment.[411] But Muslim and Jewish religious authorities continue to cite Schulze among the proofs of the superiority of their techniques for sparing animals suffering. Even the Muslim Student Association of Miami University does so.[412]

In Summary

Defenders of both kosher and halal methods of slaughter each say the following of their respective procedures:

1. The procedure is the most humane and painless there is for the animal;

2. The procedure allows the best possible bloodletting;
3. Ritual meat is healthier.

These two procedures are still strongly contested by the majority of the independent scientific community. They incarnate conceptions radically anchored in the past, rejecting modern ethical and humanistic values. Logic and scientific research have little purchase on dogmas transmitted by fundamentalist movements and their business collaborators except when the industry attempts to justify itself. And there, precisely, is the rub: he who uses pseudo-scientific arguments gets answered by scientific arguments. And the arguments in favor of ritual slaughter instantly fall to pieces.

CHAPTER FOUR

DENYING THE OBVIOUS WITH A SMOKESCREEN

Whenever the cruelty of ritual slaughter is denounced, a barrage of public statements and "academic"-style publications instantly pours forth, especially from well-organized Jewish lobbies, to defend the indefensible. It is a battlefield: ranged on one side is an alliance between Jewish and Muslim fundamentalist religious authorities and the kosher/halal meat industries, reinforced with the political and scientific allies they have purchased (or subsidized); and on other side a configuration of veterinarians, independent scientific researchers, animal defenders, consumer associations and the few rare public figures with the courage to get involved.

Among the best-known paid consultants of this international industry are Joe M. Regenstein and Temple Grandin. Also among the star referents we may cite the late professor of veterinary medicine Wilhelm Schulze, Rabbi Israel Meir Levinger and the Jewish cardiologist at the Imperial College of London Stuart D. Rosen as well as the doctor of avian pathology Jawad Hidmi. It is striking that Schulze (a specialist in pigs), despite contesting the validity of his own tests comparing conventional and religious slaughter of calves and sheep carried out 1974-78 at the University of Hannover, is still cited to prove the supposed "humanity" of ritual slaughter (as we have already mentioned). Worse, his study was even brandished in the British Parliament in 2014 by Labor Deputy Yasmin Qureshi[413], who was accusing a tabloid of prejudice in its approach to the debate over halal and kosher meat—a discredited study![414]

The overwhelming number of studies proving the cruelty of slaughter without stunning and the non-superiority of bloodletting put organizations such as B'nai B'rith, the Anti-Defamation League, Shechita UK and Unstunned Halal on auto-pilot. Ever on the defensive, they can count on an army of propagandists and broadcast texts aiming to demonstrate their "immense concern" for animal welfare. The goal, of course, is to lead the public to believe this is really the case, or at least, to maintain confusion.

A Rabbi with "Flexible" Opinions

Rabbi Israel Meir Levinger directed the kashruth department of the Central Council of European Rabbis.[415] It is difficult to give him much credit since the astonishing support he gave in 2004 to the American Agriprocessors slaughterhouse and its director Sholom Rubashkin following reports of unspeakable atrocities committed in the course of kosher slaughter by PETA, an organization devoted to the protection of animals.[416] Here are some extracts from Agriprocessors press releases:

> Rabbi Dr. I. M. Levinger, one of the world's foremost experts on animal welfare and kosher slaughter (schechita), today called schechita practices at the Agriprocessors plant "professional and humane." Dr. Levinger, a Veterinary Surgeon and Physiologist, made his remarks at the end of an intense 2-day review of schechita practices and humane animal treatment at the plant at which he observed the schechita of more than 150 animals. "In the process of handling the animals prior to schechita, care was taken to lead the animal into the pen in a most humane manner. The schechita process was performed swiftly and correctly." "The rabbis performing schechita impressed me as experts in their profession. The cut was done in an expeditious manner, cutting the trachea and esophagus, and severing the carotid arteries and jugular veins. It is my impression that schechita in this facility is performed in accordance with the highest standards of kosher handling. The behavior of the animals seem to be in accordance with the observations recorded in my book Schechita in the Light of The Year 2000."[417]

One observer remarked with irony:

1. Rabbi Dr. Levinger is said to have seen the slaughter of some 150 animals. Rubashkin's communiqué does not say whether they were all cattle or a mix of bovids and birds;

2. During the two days Dr. Levinger spent at Agriprocessors, 1000 ruminants and tens of thousands of chickens were killed. So he only saw a tiny fraction of them;
3. Dr. Levinger was invited (and his expenses no doubt quietly paid by) Rubashkin. Rubashkin, who knew when he was visiting, was able to prepare the site in advance. Genuine auditing always takes place without notice and takes much longer;
4. Above all, Dr. Levinger was only able to speak of what happened during those two days and not what happened a month before or after;
5. In short, Dr. Levinger's evaluation has no bearing on PETA's accusations and Rubashkin's misdeeds;
6. He does not say a word about Rubashkin's violations of USDA rules, which are respected by other Kosher establishments;
7. That Levinger allowed Rubashkin to use his name in this way without clearly specifying that his comments could only apply to events occurring before December 20-21 2004 is troubling and leaves in serious doubt his status as an independent expert;
8. Dr. Levinger also took the opportunity to promote his book.[418]

Bruce Friedrich of PETA remarked as follows on Levinger's visit: "This is as absurd as if a serial killer invited you to his house to observe that 'he wasn't killing anyone.' Obviously Agriprocessors are able to act correctly—our point is that they could have done things correctly, but did not—that is why their acts are illegal. A criminal can easily start obeying the law suddenly, but that does not excuse his crimes."[419]

Speaking of crimes, let us recall that Sholom Rubashkin, who was supposed to be in jail until 2033 for hiring illegal immigrants as well as for bank fraud, had his sentence commuted by US President Donald Trump on December 2017. Many Orthodox Jews were angered by Rubashkin's 27-year prison sentence. Having a group of supporters within both political parties, Jewish lobbies succeeded in their defense of Rubashkin.[420]

Although there is nothing to indicate he has been present at any kosher slaughter in his life, cardiologist Stuart Rosen of the pressure group Shechita UK mounts the barricades as soon as a critical opinion is heard.[421] On October 23, 2014, Rosen publicly "sent packing" 14,000 British veterinarians united against slaughter without prior stunning.[422] The group Shechita UK, whose spokesman Rosen is, defines itself as "a vast movement which unites representatives of the Board of Deputies of British Jews, the National Council of Shechita Boards, the Union of Orthodox Hebrew Congregations and the campaign to protect shechita, as well as the delegates of all kashruth agencies in the United Kingdom. Shechita UK was founded with the purpose of diffusing information on the Jewish religious method of humane slaughter of animals for food, and to dissipate the myths and falsehoods which have too often been used to attack Jews and their religion."[423] And who do we find "testifying" on behalf of the group on its website? Grandin and Regenstein![424]

Although this is how they present themselves, to believe Joe Regenstein and Temple Grandin are dedicated to animal well-being would be as ridiculous as believing that tobacco industry spokesmen give priority to public health. Rarely will one find two individuals as assiduous in refining the logistics of ritual slaughter on a grand scale while attacking all researchers who disagree with them. Professor in the department of Food Science at Cornell and member of the program of Jewish Studies, Regenstein is at the service of the great meat conglomerates. His academic page[425] speaks for itself:

> My primary outreach program is the Cornell Kosher and Halal Food Initiative, (CKHFI) a unique program that provides significant impact to its stakeholders. The goal of CKHFI is to help the food industry be successful in providing kosher and halal foods to consumers worldwide. There are several key stakeholders. In practical terms, much of the outreach is extended to this group [the food industry], sometimes as individual companies and sometimes through associations such as the AMI (American Meat Institute).[426]

Regenstein's two principle research areas are the production of gelatin from fish skin and scales, the growth of the kosher and halal sheep and goat markets, and the application of glatt kosher norms demanded by ultra-orthodox Jews:

> The issue of lung health constitutes a major obstacle to kosher market expansion in New York State, and must be resolved to open up new markets to benefit farmers, consumers, ethnic/religious minorities, and other consumer groups. We will use ultrasound on live animals to determine lung health followed by post-slaughter inspection of these lungs, seeking to improve animal lung health and, eventually, to be able to screen out animals that will not pass the kosher lung inspection.[427]

116

Regenstein's teaching focus is made to measure for serving fundamentalist goals: to lead students:

1) to think critically about scientific facts and how they must be examined and understood as part of a larger view of the world, even when the facts seem counter-intuitive to students' experience or expectation; 2) to be able to incorporate knowledge and understanding of diversity as it affects consumer food choices; this requires understanding how a manufacturer might respond to resulting consumer choices based on religious law.[428]

Of course, Regenstein never admits that his objectivity might be compromised by the financing he receives from the industry. But he never misses an occasion to cast doubt on the researchers who contradict his theories. In a text cosigned by Temple Grandin, he says "it is important that scientists must be absolutely objective when evaluating these practices from an animal welfare standpoint. Evaluation of religious slaughter is an area where many people have lost scientific objectivity. This has resulted in biased and selective reviewing of the literature. Politics have interfered with good science."[429]

In other words, nearly all researchers are "subjective" apart from themselves. In a report[430] which aimed to oppose the banning of ritual slaughter planned by the Dutch legislature, Regenstein attack's Gibson's New Zealand study to the effect that animals feel pain during slaughter: "Words like suffering are also thrown in to add a little drama. This is a word that needs to be defined and requires a great deal more research. It is not the same as 'pain.' [...] Presumably the authors are hoping that the less scientific readers will only read the summary and/or conclusions." Also in the same report, Regenstein expresses nothing but contempt for the work of the Dutch researchers of the Animal Science Group:

The use of the term "ritual rites" suggests a bias. These are methods of religious slaughter and the use of that term is preferred so as not to start by biasing the discussion. The second paragraph assumes and takes as a given that there is "fear" and "pain." Again if this is a scientific review, this should not be stated as a given and makes one question the sincerity (and completeness) of the review. The definitive statement that un-stunned slaughter is "at odds with animal welfare" is again a statement that makes the review less than credible. The reference to the veterinary community is inappropriate. Ethics or morality is a branch of philosophy dealing with "reason" – so it is fine for anthropomorphic and pet centered veterinarians to feel that something is wrong, but that does not relieve them of their scientific obligation to do so objectively with proper evaluation of the data. Again the review seems to want to be sure to tell you that the data supports these inaccurate conclusions. The use of the word "suffer" again is prejudicial. Both the Jewish and Muslim religions are people-centered. The final data takes the worst case numbers and muddles the words unconsciousness with insensitivity. And it also immediately assumes that the animals are experiencing pain. All of this detracts from the credibility of the work. The high level of aneurysms suggests that the person doing the cutting needs some training. The high level of vocalization again suggests that these investigators had significant problems with their system. So again, how valuable is any data reported?

But that animals may really have suffered because of the method of slaughter used does not even touch Joe Regenstein: The final conclusion clearly was the goal of the work, i.e., to recommend stunning." Whereas his own conclusion, "preaching non-insensibilization," was the only goal of his report seeking to pressure Dutch legislators to reject the law against ritual slaughter passed by the legislature. Unfortunately, this is the type of expert witness who influences the politics of decision making in the era of "globalization."

Temple Grandin and the
"Inhumane" Instrumentalization of Animals

A consultant for the kosher/halal meat industry, Temple Grandin, Professor of Animal Science at the University of Fort Collins, Colorado, was diagnosed with "high-functioning autism" at the age of four. The owner of a consulting firm, she designs cattle-breeding equipment. At first, she was strongly anti-shechita, while today she is called a "specialist" in the Talmudic treatise *Chullin*[431] (even without being Jewish[432]).

Grandin and her colleague Regenstein affirm that ritual slaughter is painless when properly practiced with good, competitive equipment. An animal "zens out" before being cut, and being held in a halter unable to move is the very quintessence of an "easy death."

In her critique of the book *Animals in Translation*, written by Grandin, Karen Davis, President of the United Poultry Concerns, expresses serious reservations as to the consultant's credibility in the matter of animal well-

118

being. Emphasizing that autistic persons are disconnected from the emotional states of others, she asks how Grandin can interact with animals with complex social and communicational abilities. What should we think of her inability to feel empathy? Does she really fit the profile for her line of work? She finds that Grandin is a dubious witness when she attributes the aggressiveness of chickens to "genetic flaws" without even mentioning the role of cages: "Grandin says nothing to enlighten the uninformed reader that the pecking to which she refers is abnormal behavior brought on by caging, crowding, boredom, filth, fear, disease, intentional food deprivation and other destructive factors of human origin."[433] Davis throws Grandin off her pedestal completely:

> Grandin's proclaimed paucity of emotion, compartmentalized emotions, and subnormal sensitivity to pain, her focus on technical fixes and disconnected brain functioning, her contention that slaughterhouse cattle don't know they're going to die and claim of being unable to watch horror movies because the images stay in her conscious mind (because she doesn't have an "unconscious" like normal people, she says), while having a stomach for the slaughterhouse but no stomach for vegetarianism (it makes her sick, she says, and isn't part of our "animal natures," [...] dents the notion that she's an animal-friendly "savant."[434]

For decades, Grandin has refined the procedures of an increasingly insane industrial logistics, not because of her autism, but because she incarnates the normal societal schizophrenia of love of animals compatible with the whole gamut of possible abuse, as long as everything is done "humanely" (sic).

Davis cites Matthew Scully, who marvels at how Grandin tries to balance her purported empathy for animals with "her consistent support of intensive farming and its economic objectives."

The woman who designed a third of the equipment used in the US is an ideal supporter of the kosher slaughterhouse industry, even if she has not managed to introduce the least audit surveillance video into them.[435]

But Grandin sometimes gets out of line by connecting the 24.5 cm halal slaughter knife with suffering of slaughtered calves observed in Gibson's 2009 New Zealand study.[436] An unconscious lapse or implicit recognition of the cruelty of ritual slaughter?

In the Name of "Science"

Unstunned Halal was an Islamic pressure group led by Dr. A. Majid Katme, Director of the Islamic Medical Association and advisor to the Muslim Council of Great Britain, Dr. Yunes Teinaz, spokesman for the London Mosque and Dr. Abbas Adel, microbiological consultant notably for the British Ministry of Health. On the organization's website, Dr. Jawad Hidmi, member of the American Meat Sciences Association, attacked the prohibition against slaughter without stunning passed in 2011 by the Dutch Legislature, offering a good example among many others of the type of specious arguments used by defenders of ritual meat:

The following comments will support the scientific point of view and will be based only on the scientific explanation and evidence, away from religion, belief and doctrine. [...] I'm not either a man of religion or a man of politics but a man of science. [...] Let us now determine to what extent it [ritual slaughter] can be painful (cruel). How much painful [sic] is the method, only Allah the Creator of the animal (and the animal which undergoes the operation while being disposed) knows.[437]

And it is this same "man of science" who, in an article based upon sharia law, puts Islamic slaughter among the "Miracles of the Koran":

> In this research we are going to unveil some of the treasures, jewels and pearls in miraculous sea of the Holy Quran of which its wonders and miracles that don't stop to chase us [sic]. It was scientifically proved undoubtedly that the Holy Quran spoke about many scientific and universal facts 14 centuries ago before they were discovered and known by modern science. We will live through this research with some facts the Holy Quran told us about or guided us to follow them and we will see that Quran spoke about these facts in a very scientific accurate language using Court of linguistic and very precise scientific expressions, proving the Quran's God's true words, and that prophet Mohammad didn't speak of his own accord but was inspired and dedicated by God's words and blessing. In this research I have chosen only one topic of the several topics of the miraculous nature of the Holy Quran which exceeded more than 1000 miraculous topics and it is about "the Islamic method of slaying animals (*Zabihah Halal*) & Human health" which coincides with my field of specialization. *Al-Zabihah* is the method of bleeding the animal. Less painful but very much like the bleeding of a donor (unlike the latter, the

animal is bled to death). [...] To consider that the animal suffers appreciable pain is, in my opinion, quite absurd.[438]

The hitch is that a good part of the scientific proof to which Jawad Hidmi refers rests on the discredited experiments of Wilhelm Schulze: the best proof of an author's lack of credibility! And each year hundreds of millions of intelligent and sensitive creatures are on the receiving end...

CHAPTER FIVE

MYTHS AND FACTS

The Need for Safeguards against Abuse

Well-being is a social question: it is society which, as with human health, defines what is acceptable and inacceptable and which at least in part establishes a hierarchy of priorities. – Donald Broom

In 1959, as mentioned earlier in this work, Canada adopted a law on humane slaughter establishing that an animal must be rendered insensible before being bleed so that it dies without regaining consciousness. This measure was integrated into the Meat Inspection Law which, however, reiterated an exemption from insensibilization if the animal is "slaughtered according to a ritual in conformity with Jewish or Islamic Law" or put to death "by the rapid, complete and simultaneous slicing of the jugulars and carotids so as to lose consciousness immediately (Article 77).

Quebec includes this exception in article 6.4.2.2 of its Food Regulations. This dispensation is based on what the practitioners of ritual slaughter have said for centuries about their respective procedures:

1. It is the most humane and painless there is for the animal;
2. It assures the best possible bloodletting;
3. Ritual meat is healthier and better for you.

An attentive review of the declarations and writings to this effect shows that all the arguments used recur from one country to another. On the other side, what is most striking is the overwhelming convergence of opinion

123

among independent researchers to the effect that all animals without exception should be stunned before slaughter because of the unnecessary suffering caused by slaughter without stunning.

We share with animals the same physiological mechanisms and biochemical substances for pain perception. Rare are our occasions for reflecting on the seriousness of what this implies. The question is not whether there are techniques worse than ritual slaughter, but whether ritual slaughter itself is admissible. Let us recall that it was originally based on the prohibition against consuming blood "enacted" by Yahweh or Allah as reported in the Torah and the Koran. From there, commentators or interpreters of the following centuries have extrapolated by ruling that for this purpose it is necessary to slaughter animals without stunning, and have erected this into an inescapable dogma. This was perhaps the best way of proceeding in those superstitious ages. According to interpreters of the Koran and the Hadith, blood is the vehicle for sickness, indeed, a deadly poison. And yet there has never in the history of Europe or America been any case of death from the consumption of blood pudding.

In the Larousse French dictionary, the word fundamentalist is defined as: "Attitude and disposition of certain religious believers who in the name of an uncompromising respect for tradition, refuse all development." An attitude well-illustrated by Professor of Jewish History Geoffrey Alderman:

> Shechita and the rules of kashruth concern faith and have absolutely nothing to do with health. Of course, we Jews do not have the right to consume blood (cf. e.g., Deuteronomy 12: 23), but this has nothing to do with the way we kill livestock. [...] We practice shechita, we avoid certain foods and we circumcise our male children because we believe these are divine commands. No other form of justification is necessary or appropriate.[439]

This is correct. The practice of Judaism rests on respect for the commands of God called *mitsvot,* which concern the duties of man toward God, his neighbors, and himself. Eating kosher belongs to the obligations toward God.

Kashruth belongs to the category of *mitsvot* called *chukim* (rules the reasons for which are beyond human understanding). Issuing from divine command, this dietetic regime whose purpose cannot be made explicit is followed simply because it has been commanded. The Islamic counterpart to *mitsvot* is sharia. But if religious beliefs are beyond discussion, how does one explain the media bombardment of "scientific" justifications by the promoters of ritual slaughter? The Jewish surgeon Stuart Rosen, a great promoter of shechita in the UK[440], wins the prize for bashing:

> It is likely that one reason for the clamor for stunning in certain quarters is confusion of an aesthetic nature. Characterization of Shechita as 'cutting an animal's throat', with descriptions of blood spurting from the neck or of the late muscular spasms, are unattractive, to say the least. However, to the uninitiated, coronary artery bypass surgery is also visually unappealing! In dealing with an issue as important as the potential suffering of animals, it is unacceptable that superficial aesthetic considerations should be allowed to cloud the argument.[441]

But a bypass is performed under general anesthesia: a capital difference! So poor an argument is surprising, coming from a cardiologist. Another reason for us to question the rationality of the three arguments which try to get us to swallow ritual slaughter in the strict sense, where the bloodlet animals die without stunning and fully conscious.[442]

Allegation no. 1:
"The most humane and painless procedure for the animal"

Myth: Rapid slicing of the carotid arteries, jugular veins, trachea and esophagus [but not the vertebrae or spinal cord] by means of a very sharp blade instantly induces massive hemorrhaging. Since the brain is no longer being fed with blood and oxygen, the animal very rapidly loses consciousness without having time to feel pain. Endorphins (natural opioids) are also secreted, so that the animal dies in a sort of "natural anesthesia."

Facts: The deep transversal cut to the animal's neck affects vital tissues such as the skin, muscle, trachea, esophagus, carotid arteries, jugular veins and the vagus and phrenic nerves. It is a major wound initiating a deluge of sensory information to the brain.[443] The pain messages captured by the muscular nociceptors first pass through the spinal cord before being relayed to the encephalon (limbic system). Of course, the lack of oxygen to the brain ends by rendering the animal unconscious—after a painful agony of 2-14 minutes, since the spinal column has been kept intact during slaughter.

This conclusion was corroborated in 2006 by the Federation of Veterinarians of Europe: "slaughter without stunning delays loss of consciousness for several minutes."[444] The delay is linked to the fact that thousands of animals bleed slowly because of pseudoaneurysms which occur in a large percentage of them, a phenomenon known as the ballooning effect. The following conditions lead to slower bloodletting:

> The sliced artery is occluded by the environing tissue (the artery is elastic and can go back in its sheath of conjunctive tissue after the cut); blood platelets collect at the end of the cut artery (this involves the rapid production of a clot which can block the artery); and the artery can be affected by an annular spasm.[445]

These three factors have a tendency to restrict the flow of blood from the wound and can cause swelling at the extremities of the cut vessel. Blood invades the sheath of conjunctive tissue bordering the artery, whose ends may balloon within five seconds of the cut. Several studies have shown that this ballooning effect is common (occurring in up to 40% of cases).[446]

In short, blood coagulates at the extremities of the sliced carotid arteries, which contract. These "stoppers" diminish the flow of blood from the carotids and slow the loss of blood pressure necessary for the deactivation of the sensitive cortex. The brain continues to be irrigated by the two vertebral arteries, which are a back-up circuit in case the carotids are cut. So the animal feels pain during the whole interval preceding its cerebral death. According to the work of D. K. Blackmore, Professor in the Department of Veterinary Pathology and Public Health at the University of Massey, New Zealand: "calves remain standing up to 135 seconds after their throats are cut, and up to 385 seconds pass before they cease trying to get back on their feet. Despite the slicing of the carotid arteries and jugular veins, three calves out of four are still breathing after 11.6 minutes. Lambs pant for 3.8 minutes after the cut. An ox killed according to the Jewish method pants sporadically for seven minutes after having its carotid arteries, jugular veins, trachea and esophagus sliced.[447]

Dr. Haluk Anil, scientific consultant at the University of Cardiff, has observed that five minutes may pass before calves whose throats have been cut cease trying to get up. He and his team observed arterial occlusions in 50% of calves killed according to the halal method. Among some calves, blood flow via the cerebral arteries maintained itself at one third of its normal level for nearly three minutes. So the animals do not lose consciousness immediately. Some animals get up and even travel a certain distance before collapsing.[448] Researchers C. J. Newhook and D. K. Blackmore have observed a delay of between 2 and 43 seconds before loss of consciousness among sheep.[449] The delay is shorter for sheep because of certain anatomical peculiarities: "Ruminant brains are fed blood via the vascular network called rete mirabile, which receives branches coming from the carotids and vertebral arteries. Among bovids, an extra anastomosis can sometimes inject blood into the rete mirabile and the brain itself after bloodletting, which is not the case with sheep or goats."[450]

In 2009, the researcher T. J. Gibson and his team arrived at the following conclusions:

> Our tests demonstrated that calves suffer during slaughter. Our data indicate that cattle aspirate (inhale) blood coming from the lungs in the course of kosher and halal slaughter. The cattle are kept in an upright position. The author also observed aspiration of blood in the course of ritual slaughter. In his opinion, this aspiration of blood is especially susceptible of constituting a major issue of animal well-being, because bovids lose sensibility (consciousness) more slowly than sheep (Baldwin, 1971; Blackmore, 1984). So the period of aspirating blood is longer for bovids than for ovines. Sheep lose sensibility more quickly because of anatomical differences between their blood vessels and those of bovids (Baldwin, 1971; Baldwin and Bell, 1963).[451]

Extract from a report by the Scientific Group on Animal Health and Well-being written at the request of the Commission on the Humaneness of Methods of Stunning and Slaughtering Animals: "Cuts intended to provoke rapid bleeding involve significant destruction of tissue in areas with many nerves. The rapid loss of blood pressure which follows hemorrhaging is clearly felt by the conscious animal and involves terror and panic. The conscious animal also suffers when its blood spreads to its trachea."[452] And here is what the expert report of the National Institute of Agronomic Research (NIAR) published in December, 2009, has to say:

> The transection of the tissues and principle blood vessels of the neck during ritual slaughter provokes cerebral responses due to the painful stimulation caused by the transection of tissues and not the diminution of cerebral irrigation. The expert scientific report on animal pain published by NIAR in December 2009 mentions times to loss of consciousness in bovines superior to two minutes for 18% of ritually sacrificed animals, sometimes rising as far as 14 minutes. For calves and adult bovines great

127

variation in loss of consciousness is observed, with extremes of 8 seconds and 14 minutes, which can be explained by the formation of pseudoaneurysms in the longest delays. Field studies show that, after Muslim (halal) and Jewish (shechita) slaughter, the formation of pseudoaneurysms is observed in 17% and 18% of bovines respectively.[453]

The report by the scientific group of the European Food Safety Authority clearly specifies that bovines and calves lose consciousness relatively slowly after slaughter. It is not rare to see a cow or bull agonizing over two minutes after having its throat cut. The animal tries to breath, to get up.[454] "It is a hard sight to bear," write the authors of the report by the Permanent Committee for Coordinating Inspections (COPERCI), *Field Inquiry on Halal*, published in September, 2005.[455] One may also consult *"Animals Feel the Pain of Ritual Slaughter"* by Craig Johnson, a review of the 2009 New Zealand study. It was financed by the UK and New Zealand Ministries of Agriculture.[456]

The convenient hypothesis of "natural anesthesia" so dear to Joe Regenstein[457] and Stuart Rosen[458] does not hold up either. In both humans and animals, pain signals prompt the avoidance of potentially dangerous or lethal situations. According to Pieter Kat, all mammals have nociceptors, sense neurons present in the parts of the body which feel internal and external pain signals [muscles, vital organs, etc.]: [These sense neurons] contain two types of axon: one which carries signals to the central nervous system rapidly (20 meters per second) and another slower one (2 meters per second). Pain is perceived in two tempos—first a vivid initial signal sent by the rapid axons, followed by a persistent pain sent by the slower axons. Since the endorphins released into the blood cannot reach the brain in great quantity due to the blood-brain barrier, their physiological anti-pain role is far from assured. [...] What endorphins do, (the word comes from endogenous and morphine) among other things, is to interact with opiate receptors in the brain to reduce the perception of pain. Anyone who has suffered serious wounds knows how ineffective endorphins can be! Humans do not secrete endorphins weaker than other mammals; far from it, they are all nearly identical peptide hormones. It is not surprising that severely wounded persons need strong doses of morphine for relief. Other mammals, like humans, have endorphin hormones which lessen their pain but are far from dissipating it when the animal is wounded, stressed and frightened.[459]

Facts corroborated by Matthieu Ricard: "A massive discharge of endorphins by the brain is the very sign that an animal is subject to intense pain and that the body is trying to minimize its impact."[460]

Conclusion: The proofs that allegation no. 1 is dishonest are overwhelming. The condition associated with the exception to article 77 of the Canadian and Quebec Provincial Laws (i.e., if the animal is slaughtered according to a ritual in conformity with Jewish or Islamic Law, or put to death "by rapid, complete and simultaneous slicing of the jugulars and carotids so that it loses consciousness immediately") prove an impossibility because of the very nature of the procedure employed. This exception should, therefore, be withdrawn.

Allegation no. 2:
"The procedure which assures the best possible bloodletting"

Myth: Slaughter without prior insensibilization is the best way to assure complete bloodletting of the animal, and consequently promotes healthier meat. Slicing of the vagus nerve involves an acceleration of heart rate and breathing, and thus a faster and more complete evacuation of blood. The convulsions which occur are essential to the process of bloodletting ["somewhat like a sponge being wrung out," according to some propagandists].

Facts: In the conventional method of slaughter, the stunned animal is also entirely emptied of blood. That is why it is suspended to allow the draining of residual blood by gravity, otherwise the meat could not be kept during the 8-15 days' refrigeration necessary for its maturation before being put on the market. The volume of blood taken from the animal is exactly the same.

Here are the principle studies corroborating these facts:

In 1966, A. W. Kotula and N. V. Helbacka measured the volume of blood from chickens slaughtered in different ways. Birds killed according to the Jewish rules did not lose more blood than those stunned in advance (whether by electricity, gas, or stun-gun). The animals killed without stunning lost blood more quickly at the beginning, but the total volume of blood collected after 300 seconds was the same as for the pre-stunned birds.[461] Moreover, Kotula and Helbacka found that the various methods of slaughter had an effect on the distribution of blood in the carcass: "the giblets of birds which were pre-stunned contained a smaller quantity of blood than those from birds slaughtered in kosher fashion."[462] The pieces from pre-stunned birds sold to the public contained less blood than those from birds killed according to the Jewish method!

In 1968, H. E. Bywater stated that stunning does not limit the amount of blood taken from the animal and that this is easily demonstrated by the quantity of residual hemoglobin in the meat. Meat from kosher slaughterhouses can be paler than that of pre-stunned animals, but this is because in Jewish ritual slaughter the animal, trying to get its breath, will have a greater concentration of oxyhemoglobin in its blood.[463]

In 1976, D. K. Blackmore stated that in total, only half the blood drains from the carcass of sheep during slaughter, whether the animal is stunned in advance or not.[464]

In 1981, a New Zealand study of lambs by Kirton, Frazerhurst, Woods, and Chrystall concluded that the volume of blood collected in a bloodletting of 120 seconds was the same for stunned and unstunned lambs.[465]

In 1983 and 1985, the Food Research Institute declared that killing an animal before it is bled, e.g., by high-voltage electrical stunning, has no effect on the volume of blood drained from the carcass.[466]

In 2001, researcher Haluk Anil published a study comparing the speed of exsanguination and the evolution of the carcass between animals stunned with electricity and those bloodlet without stunning. The results showed that sheep electrically stunned in advance do not bleed more quickly and that rigor mortis and lowered pH occur more quickly. The author concludes that "the appearance of the meat is better for the animals that have been stunned."[467]

In 2004 and 2006 at the University of Bristol, researcher Haluk Anil and his team carried out studies comparing conventional and religious slaughter (sheep in 2004[468] and bovines in 2006[469]). They demonstrated that "the volume of blood drained from the animal and the rate of exsanguination [measured every ten seconds] are the same with or without preliminary stunning." Prof. Anil's team already demonstrated that stunning does not affect bloodletting in sheep. They did the same with bovines. They measured the quantity of blood taken from 13 bovines killed according to Muslim ritual, then killed 13 others the same way, this time with a preliminary stunning by means of electrical shock or a blow to the head with a stun-gun. "Stunning produces no difference in the volume of blood taken; consequently, this objection can no longer be used," concluded Dr. Anil, who coordinates the European Union project for examining legislative questions and animal ethics raised by religious slaughter.[470]

In 2011 and 2012, the voluminous report by Haluk Anil financed by the English Beef and Lamb Executive (EBLEX) and the Agriculture and Horticulture Development Board (AHDB) came to the same conclusion:

> These results were later confirmed by the study of Gomes Neves et al. (2009). Velarde et al. (2003) carried out similar studies in lambs and found a slight increase in blood loss after electrical stunning, rather than an improvement in blood loss by slaughter without stunning. The most recent investigation by Khalid (2011) compared exsanguination following three Halal slaughter treatments: electrical stunning, no stunning and neck cut as well as post-cut electrical stunning using a v-restraining conveyor. Both experimental and commercial trials were carried out in 440 sheep slaughtered in upright or horizontal position. They found no statistically significant differences in carcass weight and by-products or in loss of blood confirming earlier results with addition of V-restraining and also post-cut stunning to treatments tested.[471]

In 2014, Drs. Colin Brewer and Peter Osin of the Royal Marsden Hospital of London compared beef and venison which had been shot to pieces of halal and kosher beef. According to the report, there is no significant difference in the presence of blood between animals stunned by electronarcosis before slaughter and those which did not undergo electronarcosis. The presence of blood is the same in the flesh of animals slaughtered according to kosher and halal rites and animals slaughtered without any religious ritual:

> Brewer and Osin reported microscopic slides of ordinary beef and halal and kosher beef all retained similar amounts of red blood cells. [...] As reported by The Times, Osin, who comes from a Jewish family concluded: "If ritual slaughter not only causes levels of avoidable pain and distress to meat animals, but also fails in its stated purpose of removing as much blood as possible, compared with other methods, then it becomes more difficult to justify and defend." Meanwhile Brewer, also Jewish, said: "Our paper may be the first to note that even when animals are shot and then not bled for several hours, if at all, there is no more blood in their meat than after conventional or ritual slaughter."[472]

It should be noted that meat totally without blood is a scientific impossibility because of the capillaries (microscopic blood vessels). For millennia, all persons who have eaten meat, regardless of religious belief, have been consuming blood.

Allegation no. 3:
"Ritual meats are healthier and better for you"

Myth: Ritual slaughter without preliminary stunning eliminates toxins and germs from the meat. This assures adequate oxygenation of the tissues and prevents the stagnation or increase of their pH levels. The Kashruth Commission (a division of the Grand Rabbinate of Quebec) cites this in its website: "Henry Baruk responds that brutal killing as opposed to [kosher] bloodletting involves the production of acroagonin (*sic*) in the blood and tissues which may render meat more toxic."[473]

The facts: To this day there exists no scientific study demonstrating the claimed superiority of ritual meat. Here is what Anil wrote in his EBLEX report:

> Velarde et al. (2003) studied comparative effects of electrical stunning versus no stunning on meat quality in lambs. They found no significant differences in color (L*, a*, b*); muscle ultimate pH (pHu), chilling losses and carcass weights after 45 min and 24 h were not significantly different between treatments. The only effect observed by Velarde et al. was petechial hemorrhages in hearts caused by electrical stunning with 250 volts for 3 seconds. No carcasses with petechial hemorrhages, ecchymosis, hematomas or broken bones were found in either treatment. They concluded that meat quality and the incidence of hemorrhages are unaffected by head-only electrical stunning. This is in agreement with other studies by Anil et al. (2004) who also examined meat quality parameters as well as packed cell volume and carcass weights in lambs after religious slaughter without stunning or slaughter with electrical stunning in lambs. Comparing captive bolt stunning with halal slaughter without stunning, Anil et al. (2006) also found no differences between treatments in packed cell volume and meat quality parameters in cattle. In an earlier limited study, Anil et al. (1993) reported effects of preslaughter handling and halal slaughter on quality parameters including packed cell volume, pH and color in sheep and cattle. There were some increases in

pH and packed cell volume values, probably due to long transport and preslaughter handling, but no change in muscle colour.[474]

As for acroagonin, a word which comes from the Greek *akros* (supreme) and *agon* (struggle), it appears that "looking for the way electroshocks worked, Cerletti, the inventor of electroconvulsive therapy, hypothesized the existence of a group of substances of extreme defense with strengthening effects, whence the term acroagonin. These vitalizing substances were supposedly formed or augmented in the organism and especially the brain under the influence of electroshock, and more generally in a being confronted with a major trial, in particular on the threshold of death (preagony or death agony, final struggle). [....] Subsequent work has not confirmed the validity of Cerletti's hypothesis, which has since been abandoned."[475]

The method of slaughter has no effect on the taste of meat. In the end, it is the method of slaughter itself which creates the difference between ordinary and halal meat[476], except that in the former, the animal does not have its head half cut off! And the more brutal the process, the stronger the production of toxins harmful to health.

The experiment carried out by N. G. Gregory in 1998 deserves to be cited: "We saw after inoculating a mixture of ground meat and blood with bacteria that the growth of bacteria was not higher than in meat unmixed with blood."[477]

Science today has a tendency to question the consumption of animal proteins for reasons that have nothing to do with the arguments of either Islam or Judaism.

Kosher butchers can cut off all the fat they are able, there is practically as much cholesterol in the fibers of white meat as in visible fat. The regular consumption of animal proteins leads the liver to secrete too many IGF molecules, associated with the main forms of cancer as well as Alzheimer's disease.[478] Because of its strong acidity, meat leads to a diminution in bone mass and to osteoporosis. There is also an overproduction of bile acids (especially chenodeoxycholic acid) produced in the course of digestion. Bacteria of the clostridium genus are transformed in the intestine into powerful carcinogenic substances. Blood iron in meat involves the oxidation of cholesterol, which damages the blood vessels (arteriosclerosis or blockage of the arteries). It also generates compounds known as Radical Hydroxyl which can damage DNA and sabotage the activity of defense cells. The best way to diminish the risk of bacterial contaminations such as colibacillus, campylobacter and salmonella... is vegetarianism!

Several members of the Jewish community[479] (and certain progressive Muslims[480]), critical of the methods of slaughter and moved by compassion for animals, have adopted a vegetarian (or vegan) diet. Some also do so for reasons of health.

CHAPTER SIX

CRUELTY: AN IMPLICIT ADMISSION?

A Bold Attempt that Speaks for Itself

Cruelty toward animals is punished by the Canadian Criminal Code. In December 2002, the Canadian Jewish Congress (CJC), speaking also in the name of the Muslim community, delivered a memo[481] to the Standing Senate Committee on Legal and Constitutional Affairs on the subject of Bill C-10B, a proposed law to modify the criminal code (cruelty toward animals). The pro-ritual-slaughter lobbies were trembling with anxiety. Those of hunters, fishermen, trappers and agribusiness were also agitated by the possibility that the old 1892 law might have real teeth.

The CJC then tried one of the grossest prestidigitation tricks in its history. It recommended that slaughter without stunning be permanently exempted from any possibility of penal sanction based on the Law against cruelty toward animals. This is rather curious coming from religious communities that have proclaimed for centuries that their methods are the most humane possible. Ritual slaughter benefits from an exemption cast in stone and integrated into the Law on meat inspection which allows slaughter without insensibilization if the animal is "slaughtered according to a rite in conformity with Jewish or Islamic Law, or if the animal is killed by rapid, complete and simultaneous slicing of the jugulars and carotids so that it immediately loses consciousness" (Article 77).

But the lobbies had the Criminal Code in their sites…

135

Supposedly Irreproachable Techniques
in Quest of Immunity

Bill C-10B revives an old bill C-15B whose article 182.2 (formerly 182.1) was amended as follows:

> Everyone commits an offence who, willfully or recklessly, causes or, being the owner, permits to be caused unnecessary pain, suffering or injury to an animal; kills an animal or, being the owner, permits an animal to be killed, brutally or viciously, regardless of whether the animal dies immediately.

During a session of the Standing Committee on Justice and Human Rights held November 29, 2001, there occurred an exchange between Irwin Cotler, deputy from Mont-Royal and Anne McLennan, then Minister of Justice:

> Mr. Irwin Cotler (Mont-Royal, Liberal): Minister, I've received representations from members of the Jewish community and members of the Muslim community who have expressed concern to me that for example, the practice of ritual slaughter related to the laws of Kashrut in the Jewish tradition and the related Muslim practices of halal might be prejudiced, if not targeted, by this legislation.[482]

Adopted October 9, 2002 under no. C-10, the bill passed the hurdle of its first reading in the Senate October 10, 2002. But the CJC found that the revised bill did not sufficiently protect Jewish or Islamic ritual slaughter. So the CJC submitted the following two suggestions to the Committee:

> That the legislation (a) explicitly exempt Jewish and Islamic ritual slaughter from its provisions or, in the alternative, (b) mandate the requirement of the Attorney General's consent for any prosecution under the animal cruelty provisions of the Bill.

Either possibility would have granted them an exception in advance.

The Art of Saying Both a Thing and Its Opposite

First the CJC broke out the violins (Section II of the memo):

Safeguarding animals from cruelty is an important Jewish value. First articulated in the Torah (the Holy Bible), it was elaborated on and given further expression in the Talmud and subsequent Judaic law codes and to this day continues to be a very valid imperative. CJC, therefore, has been fully supportive of the spirit that has animated the introduction of legislation that would result in more effective animal protection. The organization's core concern has been to ensure that such legislation did not impinge negatively on the practice of ritual slaughter of "permissible" animals, which is so fundamental to the Jewish religion (and to the Islamic faith as well).[483]

Then the CJC dropped the "bomb." The cat was finally out of the bag:

The CJC remains troubled by the allowance for private prosecutions, notwithstanding Section 182.5 of this Act and the provisions of the Criminal Law Amendment Act, 2001, which place certain requirements on any such efforts. In CJC's view, the door remains open for malicious private prosecutions by persons or organizations intent on attacking ritual slaughter or motivated by even more nefarious aims. It also makes it possible for the inevitable attendant publicity to be exploited and imposes on those sectors of the Jewish and Muslim communities directly affected the burden of a defense.[484]

The message could not have been clearer: we know that we make animals suffer and we want to continue to do so without public knowledge.

The CJC and the Islamists must have been relieved when Bill C-10B died. But their reprieve was brief. Legislators returned to the charge in 2008.

Then Came Bill S-203...

Let us be clear: although no country in the world really protects the interests of animals independently of human interests, Canada is one of the worst in regard to legal protections for animals.[485] In 2008 one could say that it had not, for the most part, modernized its system since 1892, when the law on cruelty toward animals was written into the Criminal Code. These gaps prevent the prosecution of many persons for serious crimes against animals. And the use of the term "voluntary negligence" makes prosecution very difficult in cases of negligence.

The reception accorded Bill S-203 was stormy. Jewish and Muslim groups feared that a law with teeth in it would affect slaughter without stunning. The new law substantially increased maximal penalties and terms of imprisonment for cruelty or negligence. Apart from that, it included nothing impressive, at least nothing to seriously worry slaughterers.

The federal government adopted Bill S-203 in April 2008, modifying the Criminal Code in regard to cruelty toward animals.[486] It conserves almost all the terms and expressions of the law adopted in 1892. Law S-203 does not, however, contain any legal definition of what an animal fundamentally is. Cases of negligence must be proven planned or voluntary.

Law S-203 in brief:

Killing or wounding livestock 444. (1) Everyone commits an offence who willfully (a) kills, maims, wounds, poisons or injures cattle. Punishment (2) Everyone who commits an offence under subsection (1) is guilty of (a) an indictable offence and liable to imprisonment for a term of not more than five years; or (b) an offence punishable on summary conviction and liable to a fine not exceeding ten thousand dollars or to imprisonment for a term of not more than eighteen months or to both.

Causing unnecessary suffering 445.1 (1) Everyone commits an offence who (a) willfully causes or, being the owner, willfully permits to be caused unnecessary pain, suffering or injury to an animal or a bird; Punishment (2) Everyone who commits an offence under subsection (1) is guilty of (a) an indictable offence and liable to imprisonment for a term of not more than five years; or (b) an offence punishable on summary conviction and liable to a fine not exceeding ten thousand dollars or to imprisonment for a term of not more than eighteen months or to both.[487]

Criticism of Law S-203 was not slow to appear:

> These laws do not question institutionalized forms of animal exploitation, even if they often involve more serious and systematic forms of suffering and violence. In other words, cruelty for the sake of cruelty is forbidden, but not cruelty for profit. In general, what is considered a sociably accepted practice cannot be punished by law. The interests of animals are, therefore, only considered when they coincide with the interests of human beings. The law does not protect animals for what they are, but rather for what we decide they are, i.e., the utility one wishes to impose on them. [….] The law serves above all to protect animal exploitation rather than to protect animals themselves.[488]

138

An implicit admission of cruelty from the American kosher industry? In the United States, out of concern for transparency, the big conventional slaughterhouses submit to video audits in real time transmitted by internet to independent firms. All American kosher slaughterhouses without exception have refused the installation of surveillance cameras. Even the famous consultant Temple Grandin, so close to the kosher meat industry, deplores this fact and even suggests that the public ought to be able to see what is happening there.[489] In general, when one has nothing to reproach oneself with, one has nothing to hide.

CONCLUSION

THE TREE THAT HIDES THE FOREST

When it comes to money, everyone is of the same religion.

-Voltaire

Obviously, people, organizations and entrepreneurs perceived one day the potential profit they could draw from the interpretation of religious demands applied to the industrial sphere. From their uncertain beginnings, these market niches grew to generate annual income in the hundreds of billions of dollars. Even multinationals such as Campbell, Nestlé and Cadbury have climbed on the gravy train, to which new cars are constantly being added. The rails are well-oiled by neoliberalism and globalization, and one wonders just where they will lead.

The merchandising of kosher and halal is difficult to analyze critically, provoking raised shields as soon as it is approached, because it represents a religious takeover which does not admit this is what it is. It masks what it really is, viz., an inexhaustible series of extrapolations erected into a system. It is precisely this denial which renders the phenomenon so difficult to approach.

Is the commercial exploitation of norms which accord precedence to divine over human laws issued from Roman Canon Law a symptom of something more serious? The precedent set by kosher marketing was succeeded by that of halal based on Islamic Law, which is clearly harmful in view of the project of conquest with which it is associated. Our intensive business partnerships with the oil monarchies of the Gulf and other Islamic countries are so much flirting with the enemy, who subsidize a swarm of mosques, schools, cultural and community centers which serve as vectors for fundamentalism. In the course of testimony before the US Senate in 2003, Alex Alexiev, a senior member of the Center for Security Policy, estimated that from 1975 to 2002 Saudi Arabia spent more than $70 billion to spread its radical vision of Islam across the world. Among the beneficiary organizations are the Muslim Students Association of the US and Canada (MSA) and the Islamic Society of North America (ISNA)[490], tied to the Muslim Brotherhood and to the introduction of halal certification in Canada.

Allied with the Brotherhood in Egypt, the very wealthy Wahhabi Emirate of Qatar also spends billions annually all over the world. Several Canadian Universities receive funds from the Qatar National Research Fund[491], including McGill in Montreal[492]. This foundation appears to support the totalitarian positions of Muslim Brotherhood ideologue Youssef Qarawadi.[493] In March 2012, the Institute of Islamic Studies of McGill University received a gift of $1,250,000 from the State of Qatar.[494] Kuwaiti money has circulated as far as Quebec, as the Kuwait News Agency reported April 2, 2014 with regard to $70,671 donated to the Islamic Secondary School Le Savoir, apparently tied to the Muslim Brotherhood.[495]

The University of Montreal is among the partners of the Saudi organization known as the King Abdullah Bin Abdulaziz International Center for Interreligious and Intercultural Dialogue (KAICIID) established in Vienna, Austria[496], whose mission is to promote religious tolerance. One of the most intolerant States in the world as regards religion, Saudi Arabia[497], is giving millions to a Center dedicated to respect for diverse beliefs and interreligious dialogue: a consummate bit of gaslighting! In January 2015, Austrian Chancellor Werner Faymann found it inacceptable that the organization did not denounce the prison sentence and lashing of the Saudi blogger Raïf Badawi (who promotes interreligious dialogue!) and stated that it should be closed. But when Riyadh threatened to move the seat of OPEC (based in Vienna since 1965), the Austrian government backed down.[498] The Saudi initiative tended to turn attention away from abuses committed in the kingdom itself and to encourage nations to adopt laws prohibiting any criticism of Islam (blasphemy laws).[499] It is the West they are aiming at. And the anathema used to muzzle the slightest note of dissent is "Islamophobia." One of the current advisers of the KAICIID is

Canadian Professor Patrice Brodeur, who also presided over the International Colloquium *"Halal in all its forms. Issues of halal consumption in the West and in the context of a Muslim minority: norms, objects, actors, issues, discourse and living together"* held at the University of Quebec at Montreal October 24-25, 2012. Among the participants we may cite Tariq Ramadan[500], who recognizes the intellectual leadership of Youssef al-Qarawadi[501], spiritual guide of the Muslim Brotherhood, and Prof. Kabir Hassan, an expert on halal financing from the University of New Orleans. During the colloquium, Joe Regenstein, Director of Cornell University's Kosher and Halal Food Initiative gave a lecture, *"Ritual Slaughter and Animal Well-Being: Is Ritual Slaughter Inhumane? A Scientific Point of View."*[502] A cozy solidarity prevailed.

Dr. Salim Mansur, a Muslim native from India who teaches at the University of Western Ontario, testified on December 8, 2014 to the Standing Senate Committee on National Security and Defense assessing security threats facing Canada:

> The vast majority of Muslim immigrants into Canada come from places that might best be described as a "fear society," and they cannot be reached through the portals of mosques and mosque-related institutions. The reason is simple. Most mosques here, as in the Muslim world, are incubators of Islamism. This might shock you, but this is where the problem is, and I can speak from my own experience, and any legitimacy given to them as a matter of community or political outreach only further entrenches the practitioners of Islamism disguised as religion in spreading their ideology through mosques. [...] On the discussions that take place in the mosque, senator, I brought something along with me to show you physically. I don't know how many of you have seen this book. This is not the Quran. This is the sharia. This is the standard sharia book from which discussions take place. In English it's called the Reliance of the Traveller, and *Umdat al-Salik* in Arabic. There's a whole list of texts I can point out to you that are freely circulated. I brought these along. I'm not sure if you know this particular book or have come across it. It's called *Milestones* by Sayyid Qutb, one of the founding heads of Islamism, a Muslim brother. This book, senator, is the What is To Be Done of the Muslim world, the Mein Kampf of Islamism. [503]

In 2015, a committee of the Canadian Senate turned its attention to the use made by some nonprofit organizations of certain gifts from abroad for "religious and educational activities." Without naming particular countries,

Richard Fadden, former security advisor to the Harper government, testified that money serving to promote extremist ideologies went especially to religious institutions.[504] Major General Jonathan Shaw, who served in the British Army, named Saudi Arabia and Qatar as those principally responsible for the rise of radical Islam, a breeding ground for Jihadist terror.[505] But these two countries are not the only ones that should be singled out. The policies carried out by the United States in cooperation with Pakistan at the end of the 1970s in Afghanistan (blessed with enormous reserves of natural gas and oil, and a port of entry for Central Asia)[506] set in motion a harmful process. In the context of the Cold War and coveted energy resources, the United States took to supporting some of the most fundamentalist Islamic movements on the planet.

Pipelines and Ultra-Fundamentalist Pawns: Playing with Fire

The Soviet Union invaded Afghanistan in 1979 to defend the pro-communist government in Kabul which was threatened by mujahideen rebels supported by the US. A civil war under the supervision of the two superpowers followed.[507] With the active encouragement of the CIA and Pakistani Inter-Services Intelligence (ISI), which wanted to transform the Afghan jihad into a global conflict lead by all Muslim States against the Soviet Union, over 35,000 Muslim radicals from 40 countries came to fight in Afghanistan between 1982 and 1992. Tens of thousands of others went to Pakistan to study in madrasas (Koranic schools). In sum, more than 100,000 foreign radical Muslims were directly influenced by the Afghan jihad.[508]

In fact, the ISI "served as intermediary to the CIA to furnish weapons (65,000 per year until 1987) and to organize and train the Afghan rebels. US support for the Mujahideen included the teaching of warrior values imprinted with religious extremism, the whole wrapped up in Islamic jargon, something that would prove especially fateful and harmful."[509] Subsequent events have, alas, confirmed this. Financially supported by Saudi Arabia, the Taliban took power in 1996. The US saw it as a "stable regime" favorable to the construction of pipelines to Pakistan, even if this came at the expense of the Afghan population. The Taliban "will probably develop like the Saudis," commented an American diplomat in 1997. "There will be Aramco [a consortium of oil companies which controls Saudi oil], pipelines, an Emir, no parliament and a whole lot of sharia law.

144

We can adjust to it."[510] In December 1997, Taliban representatives were invited to the Texas offices of the oil company Unocal to negotiate support of the pipeline project.[511] In the course of his testimony to a Senate Foreign Affairs subcommittee in April 1999, American congressman Dana Rohrabacher accused the Clinton Administration of conducting a clandestine policy of support for the Taliban, the most Anti-Western, Anti-Feminist, Anti-Human Rights regime in the world."[512]

Allies One Day, Mortal Enemies the Next

The US intervened in Afghanistan because the Taliban no longer furnished the stability and security required for pipeline construction. After the involvement of Osama Bin Laden in the attacks against American embassies in Kenya and Tanzania in 1998, Taliban hostility toward America grew. The great pipeline projects were suspended. In the early months of 2001, the Bush administration was planning an invasion of Afghanistan to overthrow the Taliban. But the World Trade Center attacks of September 11 (presumably financed by Saudi Arabia and al-Qaida) furnished the ideal pretext to put the already-made plans into action. The US put into place the interim Federal Government of Hamid Karzai (former consultant for Unocal), offering the stability necessary for pipeline construction. The new warlord regime of the Northern Alliance marked the return of the barbarity and brutality which had preceded the arrival of the Taliban in power—although this time the confrontations were limited to rival factions in terms of the accords established by the US and UN. The continuance of internal repression and brutality against the local population did not seem to disturb the US overmuch.[513] Tahmeena Faryal, spokeswoman for the Revolutionary Association of Women in Afghanistan (RAWA), strongly criticized the varnish of legitimacy accorded to the factions of the Northern Alliance: "Between 1992 and 1996 especially, these groups unleashed a brutal war against women, using rape, torture, kidnappings and forced marriages as weapons...."[514] But for the Bush administration, the only thing that counted was a unified federation that could guarantee a sufficient degree of stability, whatever atrocities were committed under it. On November 28, 2001, the Whitehouse published a declaration by Pres. Bush on the opening of the Caspian Pipeline Consortium's first pipeline.[515]

A few years before, in 1991, Saddam Hussein found out what it meant to go from friend to enemy[516] of a superpower. In 2003, the armed intervention of the US, Great Britain, and their allies in Iraq pitted the Sunni and Shiite Muslims against one another. Military equipment left after the retreat of American troops in 2011 were used to establish an Islamic Caliphate which, as we know, replicated itself in Syria and Libya.

Open Secrets

As revealed by Wikileaks, on December 30, 2009, Hillary Clinton (then US Secretary of State) sent a memo to America's Ambassadors posted in Saudi Arabia, Qatar, the United Arab Emirates, Kuwait and Pakistan. It is clear in this message that she knew donors from these countries were financing the activities of jihadist groups around the world, and that Saudi Arabia had been the most generous with them.[517] And if the Americans know it, one can bet the Europeans and Canadians did as well. But in this sorcerer's apprentice geopolitics in the service of oil-aristocracies and armament, only interest-based alliances count. The policies of the US and its allies favor the Saudi oligarchy, who do not want any "open" Islam around them, nor anywhere in the world. And Russia must be prevented from becoming the major supplier of oil and gas to the Old Continent, even if it means handing secular governments of the Middle East[518] over to Islamic fundamentalists[519]. The US does not want Russia teaming up with Central and Western Europe. Added to waves of replacement-level migration, the admission of Turkey into the European Community would be another nail in Europe's coffin.

Active in nearly 80 countries, the Muslim Brotherhood has a tentacular network said to be close to circles of political power. Their guru Sayyid Qutb (1906-66) serves as inspiration to several jihadist groups that dream of a world caliphate governed by sharia: "Everything must be ruled by divine authority, not by human decisions. This applies to marriage, food, dress, contracts, every form of activity and work, all social and commercial relations, all usages and customs." From this point of view, there is no way of distinguishing the profane from the sacred, the religious from the secular, Church from State, faith from politics.[520] Considered a terrorist organization, the Brotherhood is banned from the United Arab Emirates, Russia and Saudi Arabia, the latter by way of opposition to Shiite Iran, which has ties to the organization. On December 17, 2015, UK Prime

Minister David Cameron authorized publication of an official report[521] wherein the Muslim Brotherhood is perceived "as contrary to the values, national interests and national security of the State and the British people." Despite the presumed connections between the Brotherhood and jihadi terrorism, the Cameron government refused to outlaw the Brotherhood, which also operates quietly in North America. The World Muslim League (WML), devoted to the promotion of sharia, has agents in Canada and the US, Muslim Brotherhood members or Khomeinist. Some politicians publicly associate with these guys.

Oh Canada, Land of Our Collusions...

Successive governments pursue the policies of their predecessors. And for commercial enterprises, it's business as usual. The struggle against terrorism and radicalization make their entrance into media and political Newspeak while Canada hypocritically pursues lucrative sales of cutting-edge assault tanks, halal products or live sheep and goats destined to be sacrificed at annual Muslim festivities. Fundamentalism does sell: there is genuine collaboration between our commercial establishments and nations and movements dedicated to the creation of an Islamic world state. Canadian organizations affiliated or associated with the Muslim Brotherhood, including the Canadian Muslim Forum and the Islamic Society of North America (ISNA, an important halal certifier), have the support of Prime Minister Justin Trudeau, who has spoken at an ISNA meeting. On the evening after the federal election of October 19, 2015, ISNA issued a communiqué rejoicing at his victory.[522]

On November 13, 2015 (ironically the same day jihadi attacks in Paris left 130 dead), Canadian political leaders participated in the annual banquet of the Canadian Muslim Forum, a front organization for the Muslim Brotherhood.[523] By their servility and ignorance, these irresponsible politicians facilitate and banalize the propagation of radical Islam by the Muslim Brotherhood. They compromise our security just as much as do other Western leaders. As for the taxpayer, he pays for the exploding budgets allotted to defense and security because of the terrorist threat (sic). The military industrial complex thrives. One is left speechless by such cynicism, such manipulation of public opinion.

The way the Western political class swallows the banalization of sharia by business interests amounts to a shameless treason to the ideals of

147

equality that were won through fierce struggle by generations of men and women. It is a monumental slap in the face to the courageous persons who in many regions of the world resist the intolerant and retrograde diktats of their coreligionists at the risk of their lives, a dumping into the abyss of the free minds of yesterday and today who have denounced the excesses of religious fanaticism, a virtual spitting on the graves of both Muslim and non-Muslim victims, and a civilizational disavowal of mountains of efforts, suffering and fighting: for the secularity of the State, the reign of science and reason, the abolition of slavery, the equality of men and women, laws against polygamy, the criminalization of pedophilia, the recognition of the rights of homosexual persons, respect for freedom of conscience and expression, the struggle against female circumcision, the defense of animals, etc.

Greed has won out over every other consideration. Money talks, say the Americans. Salivating over favorable demographic curves, does the capitalist West dream of ever-growing exploitation of the halal niche? If so, the flame of a civilization founded on democracy and reason may ultimately burn out in a chaos of death and desolation. The value of what has been lost will greatly exceed the mountains of ill-gotten wealth.

Will the "Enlightened Civilization" Really Distinguish Herself?

Shouldn't there be public enquiries about the implementation of the halal movement in the Western countries? Doesn't any indulgence toward activities closely or distantly related to a totalitarian ideology devoted to establishing sharia amount to a direct attack on the integrity of our public institutions? Isn't this a major, even urgent, issue, before demography renders such a retrogression unavoidable?

The interests defended by the kosher and halal products industries coincide with those of communities attached to cultural and religious exemptions they have managed to obtain in various ways. The accommodations described as "reasonable" directly oppose the historic secularism model, the only guarantee of equality of treatment for all citizens.[524] This project must rest on clear positions applicable to all issues of religious intrusion into civic and public space. No violations in any sphere should have been tolerated, and should not be in future. Consider first of all of those most affected: the children undergoing an intensive religious conditioning they are not old enough to understand. Think of the schoolchildren deprived of learning the sciences or other essential secular subjects, who are not on a footing of equality with other children because of this exclusion. Think of the women put in an inferior position by macho ideologies disguised as traditions. Think of all those animals which suffer for what should rightly be called the moral bankruptcy of the West, devoted to the hegemony of business interests which relegate its noble humanistic ideal to the trash heap of history.

Alienation and fanaticism must not be confused with culture. Why must retrograde movements necessarily be tolerated? Don't articles of clothing have symbolic value in certain contexts, as Nazi armbands once did?

To believe that all traditions are equal and all citizens spontaneously act in favor of the common good without any form of coercion is one of the most naïve a priori principles imaginable. Human nature being as it is, there are contexts in which the State ought to intervene, determining the rules and obligations essential to a better common life. Minorities must be protected, of course, but not at the detriment of the most elementary common sense with regard to unreasonable practices.

The question of justifying the place of kosher and halal religious certifications in liberal democracies resembles a Rubik's cube covered with thorns: not only is it difficult to align the squares, but you don't really know how to grasp it—in short, where to start. The perspective of consumer rights constitutes in our opinion the best approach for raising the level of debate to that of principle. In fact, it is essential to set the issues in their proper context in order to evaluate whether a commercial practice is "unreasonable" or not. This role is certainly incumbent upon the State, tasked with establishing the rules of life in society and seeing to it that the same laws apply to everyone. The heritage it has to manage is difficult: multiculturalism opened a breach which was gleefully stormed by certain persons who confused pluriculturalism with legal pluralism. This is its greatest Achilles' heel and the greatest threat to the collective future of the Western civilization.

An increasing number of citizens sense that we are going backwards, sense an inarticulate unease in face of the clear gains made by obscurantism. Between indulgence and electoral opportunism, our elites succeed one another and do nothing. But there is plenty to do, if only as concerns what goes into our shopping carts, a barometer of how far Jewish and Muslim fundamentalism have intruded into our societies.

We must, quite simply, determine the following:

1. What norms are acceptable for the public sphere (commerce)?
2. What kind of practices should be relegated entirely to the private sphere?
3. What norms demonstrably contravene animal welfare?

Financial arguments should not predominate in so fundamental debate. What is at stake is nothing less than the future of our descendants. All the more so as there already exists a simple solution for signaling the absence of a specific product on labels and packaging, a neutral, universal and free logo: the pictogram. It involves no certification costs. For example, a small pint of milk in a circle with a bar across it and the words: "contains no milk products." Or a peanut and the words "no peanuts," or an ear of wheat and "gluten-free." Some companies use this effective method which has the advantage of respecting the concept of public space where everyone can feel at ease.

The other option for customers wanting to avoid pork or milk (or their derivatives) is to simply rely on the wide array of vegan products. No alcohol? Its presence is always mentioned in the listed ingredients.

An Incomparable Power Unaware of Itself

The business of gullibility is operating on a planetary scale and imposing its will. But gradually, precedents are weakening the giant's grasp. The most recent are the outlawing of slaughter without stunning in Denmark and Belgium. On May 2019, the Dutch parliament introduced for the second time a bill seeking a ban on ritual slaughter. "No religious conviction should enjoy precedence over the will of the majority of the population to avoid animal suffering," declared Walloon deputy Josy Arens.[525] Who among North American politicians would have the courage to speak in such terms?

Everywhere in the West, citizens are becoming aware of the unjust practices of these discriminatory industries. What is more a part of everyday life than the contents of a grocery cart? The last word belongs to consumers, the principle (if often unintentional) purchasers of religiously certified products.

ENDNOTES

1. Expression picked from Alain Deneault's book *Paradis fiscaux : la filière canadienne*, Montréal, Écosociété, 2014, p. 17.
2. comeandhear.com/supplement/so-daat-emet/index.html
3. daatemet.org/articles/article.cfm?article_id=119&lang=entalkreason.org/articles/gentiles.cfm
4. The kosher wine produced for Jewish Easter (Pesach) must not have been in contact with grains, bread nor dough (*chametz*).
5. today.com/id/4580443#.VyUgbYThDIU
6. journaldemontreal.com/2016/04/29/personne-ne-sait-qui-vendait-du-vin-illegal-dans-la-synagogue
7. rabbinat.qc.ca/nsite/ksr-2.html
8. academieveterinaire.free.fr/academie/les%20lois.htm
9. cie.ugent.be/aldeeb2.htm9
10. yivoarchives.org/index.php?p=collections/controlcard&id=33038
11. fr.wikipedia.org/wiki/The_Forward
12. josephjacobsadvertising.com/#!about-us/c1uk8
13. blogs.forward.com/the-arty-semite/173621/-years-of-the-maxwell-house-haggadah/#ixzz3NKQCcU9P
14. nytimes.com/1964/07/09/advertising-catering-to-the-kosher-trade.html
15. goo.gl/mjaxu
16. imjm.ca/location/1178
17. en.wikipedia.org/wiki/Simon_Glazer
18. *Ibid.*
19. goo.gl/avnWEg
20. imjm.ca/location/1178
21. imjm.ca/location/1428
22. rabbiyehudahyudelrosenberg.com/biography.htm
23. goo.gl/3twTlV
24. rabbiyehudahyudelrosenberg.com/biography.htm
25. jewishpubliclibrary.org/blog/?page_id=519
26. mimj.ca/location/1509
27. rabbiyehudahyudelrosenberg.com/biography.htm
28. imjm.ca/location/1430
29. imjm.ca/location/1178

30. goo.gl/VjwzL5

31. jewishpubliclibrary.org/blog/?page_id=519

32. rabbiyehudahyudelrosenberg.com/biography.htm

33. people.ucalgary.ca/~elsegal/Shokel/080620_KosherCrime.html

34. The *Keneder Adler* was a yiddish journal published in Montreal by Harry (Hirsch) Wolofsky for the Jewish community of Canada. The first edition was printed in 1907. The *Keneder* went out of publication in 1988.

35. jwa.org/teach/livingthelegacy/documentstudies/day-by-day-boycott-documents

36. people.ucalgary.ca/~elsegal/SEGAL.html

37. jta.org/1929/01/20/archive/grand-jury-indicts-91-for-violating-anti-trust-law-in-kosher-poultry-industry

38. kosherfest.com/history-of-kosher

39. nytimes.com/1964/07/09/advertising-catering-to-the-kosher-trade.html

40. massorti.com/Le-sens-de-la-Cacherout

41. koshervitamins.com/Boiron-Avenoc-Hemorrhoids-12-Suppositories

42. evangersdogfood.com/?p=kosher

43. pi.library.yorku.ca/ojs/index.php/cjs/article/viewFile/31319/28741

44. William Weintraub, *City Unique : Montreal Days and Nights in the 1940's and 50's*, M & S, 1996, pp. 183-202.

45. mk.ca/en

46. cerji.ca/media/mythes-et-realites-sur-la-certification-cachere

47. collections.banq.qc.ca/ark:/52327/bs66285, page 74.

48. spectrum.library.concordia.ca/7228/1/Lapidus_PhD_S2011.pdf, p. 31-32.

49. cor.ca

50. answers.com/topic/kashruth-council-of-canada

51. cjnews.com/food/loblaw-products-carry-only-cor-certification

52. cor.ca/view/180/does_it_really_need_to_be_kosher_certified.html

53. willzuzak.ca/lp/ronen09.html

54. scrollk.org/guide-to-kashrus-does-it-need-a-hechsher/

55. rabbinat.qc.ca/nsite/ksr-1.html

56. kosherimage.com/approval.html#sbt

57. kosherimage.com/e-mailings/sbt_announcement_3.html

58. thestar.com/life/2010/03/16/kosher_paper_towels_arrive.html

59. argent.canoe.ca/nouvelles/affaires/lait-cacher-des-normes-plus-severes-6082012

60. tvanouvelles.ca/lcn/infos/regional/montreal/archives/2012/11/20121101-220444.html

61. cjnews.com/news/could-kosher-food-be-cheaper

62. jewishpostandnews.ca/local/1357-corrections-to-our-previous-story-about-the-kosher-chicken-situation-in-canada

63. cjnews.com/news/politics-kashrut

64. cjnews.com/editorial/invitation-cor-our-door-still-open

65. mk.ca

66. cjnews.com/news/could-kosher-food-be-cheaper

67. massorti.com/Le-sens-de-la-Cacherout

68. *A Day in the Life of a COR Mashgiach71*: Baycrest Edition

69. cor.ca

70. mk.ca/en

71. Catherine Handfield, Montréal campus, vol. XXV, no 16, 19 avril 2006, p. 12.

72. montrealjewishmagazine.com/kosher-places

73. inspection.gc.ca/au-sujet-de-l-acia/salle-de-nouvelles/systeme-de-salubrite-des-aliments/fra/1332207100013/1332207173484

74. mapaq.gouv.qc.ca/fr/Consommation/guideconsommateur/inspection/Pages/Inspection.aspx

75. publications.gc.ca/pub?id=353161&sl=1

76. ckfsi.ca/img/uploads/_filemanager/GouvernementPressReleaseFR.pdf et ckfsi.ca/img/Minister%20Paradis%20Discours_November%204_FR1.pdf

77. ckfsi.ca/home.php

78. ckfsi.ca/img/uploads/_filemanager/CKFSInewsletterFRENCHJune.pdf

79. ckfsi.ca/home.php?lang=fr

80. ckfsi.ca/about.php

81. ckfsi.ca/img/uploads/_filemanager/CKFSInewsletterFRENCHJune.pdf [18]

82. ckfsi.ca/img/uploads/_filemanager/CKFSInewsletterFRjanvier.pdf

83. cjnews.com/news/canada/canada-wide-kosher-safety-plan-launched

84. ckfsi.ca/img/uploads/_filemanager/CKFSInewsletterFRjanvier.pdf

85. cjnews.com/news/canada/canada-wide-kosher-safety-plan-launched

86. For instance, see the 2013 and 2014 certificates of Bleuets Mistassini Ltée : bleuets-mistassini.com/File/CERTIFICAT%20KASHER.pdf, bleuets-mistassini.com/File/Kosher%202014.pdf

87. Trademark : cipo.ic.gc.ca/app/opic-cipo/trdmrks/srch/vwTrdmrk.do?lang=fra&status=OK&fileNumber=1701505&extension=0&startingDocumentIndexOnPage=1 ; Logo : cipo.ic.gc.ca/app/opic-cipo/trdmrks/srch/vwTrdmrk.do?lang=fra&status=OK&fileNumber=1701504&extension=0&startingDocumentIndexOnPage=1

88. spectrum.library.concordia.ca/7228/1/Lapidus_PhD_S2011.pdf

89. See Report by David Macdonald and Kayle Hatt, *At what Cost? The Impacts of Rushing to Balance the Budget*.

90. news.nationalpost.com/2012/04/11/budgets-cuts-mean-100-fewer-food-safety-inspectors-in-canada

91. tvanouvelles.ca/lcn/infos/regional/montreal/archives/2012/11/20121101-220444.html

92. *Ibid.*

93. inspection.gc.ca/au-sujet-de-l-acia/salle-de-nouvelles/avis-de-rappel-d-aliments/liste-complete/2012-03-01/fra/1357586660034/1357586660049

94. inspection.gc.ca/au-sujet-de-l-acia/salle-de-nouvelles/avis-de-rappel-d-aliments/liste-complete/2012-09-01/fra/1357586654660/1357586654676

95. canadiensensante.gc.ca/recall-alert-rappel-avis/inspection/2013/23199r-fra.php#!prettyPhoto

96. inspection.gc.ca/about-the-cfia/newsroom/food-recall-warnings/complete-listing/2014-05-30d/eng/1401522113750/1401522134428

97. inspection.gc.ca/au-sujet-de-l-acia/salle-de-nouvelles/avis-de-rappel-d-aliments/liste-complete/2014-06-18/fra/1403136182305/1403136197247

98. mk.ca/images/KASHRUS%20NOTICE%20STRAWBERRIES%202011.pdf

99. mk.ca/pdf/strawberries-alert.pdf

100. cjnews.com/news/kashrut-bodies-seek-greater-co-ordination-federal-inspectors

101. Fabien Deglise, *La face kasher de l'alimentation*, Protégez-vous, août 2002, p. 16.
102. Catherine Handfield, *Certification casher : sceau de confiance*, Montréal campus, vol. XXV, no 16, 19 avril 2006.
103. cjnews.com/canada/number-quebec-jews-down-census-data-indicates
104. mk.ca/en
105. cjnews.com/news/kashrut-bodies-seek-greater-co-ordination-federal-inspectors
106. blog.thesuburban.com/2013/02/an-insider.html
107. ckfsi.ca/img/uploads/_filemanager/CKFSInewsletterFRENCHJune.pdf
108. kosherfest.com/history-of-kosher
109. Catherine Handfield, *Certification casher : sceau de confiance*, Montréal campus, vol. XXV, no 16, 19 avril 2006.
110. academieveterinaire.free.fr/academie/les%20lois.htm
111. rabbinat.qc.ca/nsite/ksr-1.html
112. cor.ca/view/180/does_it_really_need_to_be_kosher_certified.html
113. ckfsi.ca/img/uploads/_filemanager/CKFSInewsletterFRjanvier.pdf
114. *Retail Intelligence : Kosher Certification*, Canadian Grocer, octobre 2012, page 22
115. gestiondelamarque.com/uploads/9/6/1/4/9614885/classement2012.qubec.rapport.sommaire.pdf
116. cjnews.com/node/83386
117. journaldemontreal.com/2015/06/28/le-nom-de-la-senatrice-hervieux-payette-a-ete-associe-a-une-firme-subventionnee
118. spectrum.library.concordia.ca/7228/1/Lapidus_PhD_S2011.pdf
119. archive.adl.org/special_reports/kosher_tax/print.html
120. *Ibid.*
121. *Ibid.*
122. en.wikipedia.org/wiki/Executive_Intelligence_Review
123. archive.org/details/TheUglyTruthAboutTheAdl_217
124. archive.org/details/AdlAnti-defamationLeagueOfBnaiBrithNewsArticles
125. archive.adl.org/special_reports/kosher_tax/print.html
126. freedomcrowsnest.wizardofthenorth.ca/viewtopic.php?t=23343#p284899
127. richmondunlimited.wordpress.com/2012/03/22/the-adl-and-the-rabbinical-kosher-excise-tax-fact-and-fiction-part-1
128. cjnews.com/news/could-kosher-food-be-cheaper
129. bazzotv.telequebec.tv/occurence.aspx?id=928&invite=385
130. news.nationalpost.com/news/canada/canadian-politics/jewish-group-accuses-parti-quebecois-candidate-of-spreading-kkk-anti-semitic-conspiracy-theory
131. adl.org/press-center/press-releases/anti-semitism-international/adl-silence-from-quebec.html
132. accommodementsoutremont.blogspot.ca/2014/04/le-silence-des-agneaux.html
133. bill613.com/news/pierre-lacerte-propagates-kosher-tax-myth
134. theamericanmuslim.org/tam.php/features/print/canadian_shia_muslim_organization. But the organization was hoisted with its own petard because the CASMO had to suppress the video following a complaint filed by the Canadian Jewish Congress.
135. That article has been taken up by a Muslim website.
136. cerji.ca/enjeux/mythes-et-realites-sur-la-certification-cachere/[Page consulted on May 13, 2015]

137. modia.org/etapes-vie/education/cashroute.html

138. adl.org/press-center/press-releases/anti-semitism-international/adl-silence-from-quebec.html

139. spectrum.library.concordia.ca/7228/1/Lapidus_PhD_S2011.pdf

140. *The Vaad Ha'ir – Montreal's Jewish Community Council – the Model of a Kehillah* (CJCCCNA/JPL/Vaad/MB 09/13/1/ History/Vaad/1930-78.) Cited by S. Lapidus in spectrum.library.concordia.ca/7228/1/Lapidus_PhD_S2011.pdf

141. Handfield, Catherine, *Certification casher : Sceau de confiance*, Montréal campus, vol. XXV, no16, 19 avril 2006, page 12.

142. blogs.timesofisrael.com/how-federation-cja-failed-the-worst-year-for-the-montreal-jewish-community/

143. cija.ca/about-us/board-of-directors/ and http://www.federationcja.org/fr/qui-sommes-nous/en-bref/

144. en.wikipedia.org/wiki/Jewish_National_Fund and http://support.jnf.org/site/TR?pg=fund&fr_id=1020&pxfid=4940

145. cerji.ca/enjeux/mythes-et-realites-sur-la-certification-cachere

146. blog.thesuburban.com/2013/02/an-insider.html

147. cjnews.com/canada/number-quebec-jews-down-census-data-indicates

148. cjnews.com/news/kashrut-bodies-seek-greater-co-ordination-federal-inspectors] and www.lesaffaires.com/monde/amerique/des-gateaux-quebecois-benis-pour-new-york/532312

149. blog.thesuburban.com/2013/02/an-insider.html

150. gestiondelamarque.com/uploads/9/6/1/4/9614885/classement2012.qubec.rapport.sommaire.pdf

151. cjnews.com/news/kashrut-bodies-seek-greater-co-ordination-federal-inspectors

152. cjnews.com/news/could-kosher-food-be-cheaper

153. cjnews.com/news/could-kosher-food-be-cheaper

154. cjnews.com/news/politics-kashrut

155. lesaffaires.com/monde/amerique/des-gateaux-quebecois-benis-pour-new-york/5323121

156. dejouerlesallergies.com/la-renaissance-des-aliments-ange-gardien

157. Handfield, Catherine, *Certification casher : Sceau de confiance*, Montréal campus, vol. XXV, no16, 19 avril 2006, page 12.

158. mk.ca/pdf/second%20cup%20notice.pdf

159. bleuets-mistassini.com

160. hassidout.org/sj/component/content/article/165-judaisme/17436-des-vetements-sans-chaatnez-lhabillement-cacher- "[…] a way of saying that Man had the right to use nature's resources at its liking but must never try to alter the order of Creation (Genesis, 2-15). Separating wool (representing the animal kingdom) from linen (representing the plant kingdom) is a symbolic reminder of that warning. Overturning the order of Creation isn't without consequences." www.kacher.fr/Kchaatnez.htm

161. islamreligion.com/fr/articles/1892

162. Halalmontreal.com/#!normeshalal/c1wee

163. fr.wikipedia.org/wiki/Youssef_al-Qarad%C3%A2w%C3%AE#cite_note-:0-2

164. www.spiegel.de/international/world/islam-s-spiritual-dear-abby-the-voice-of-egypt-s-muslim-brotherhood-a-745526.html

165. fr.wikipedia.org/wiki/Le_Licite_et_l%27Illicite_en_Islam

166. Youssef al-Qardaoui *Le licite et l'illicite en islam*, al-Qalam, 2004 », p. 45.

167. Ian Johnson, *A Mosque in Munich : Nazis, the CIA and the Rise of the Muslim Brotherhood in the West,* Mariner Books, 2010.

168. centerforsecuritypolicy.org/2003/06/26/alexiev-testifies-on-wahhabi-influence-in-us-2/

169. http://iipdigital.usembassy.gov/st/english/pamphlet/2012/07/201207028400.html #axzz45FPghCkf

170. rehmat1.com/2009/01/13/the-canadian-jew-who-believed-in-halal/

171. lexpansion.lexpress.fr/actualite-economique/isla/delice/les-secrets-du-roi-du-halal_2015190.html

172. http://www.sgs.com/en/news/2014/10/the-growth-of-the-halal-market-and-the-role-of-halal-certification

173. It is Hisham al Talib, Jamal Barzinji and Ahmed Totanji. See: http://www.discoverthenetworks.org/printgroupProfile.asp?grpid=6175

174. https://en.wikipedia.org/wiki/Islamic_Society_of_North_America#cite_note-USAvHoly-9

175. USA vs Holy Land Foundation for Relief and Development, et al, 3:04-CR-240-G (TX ND), Government exhibit Elbarasse Search1.

176. discoverthenetworks.org/printgroupProfile.asp?grpid=6175

177. freerepublic.com/focus/f-news/1146115/posts

178. isnahalal.ca/pdf/Brief%20History%20of%20Halal%20Certification.pdf

179. discoverthenetworks.org/printgroupProfile.asp?grpid=6175

180. zabihahalal.com/files/news_en/Maple_Lodge_Farms_Zabiha_Halal_Certification_ Change_1383593131.pdf

181. zabihahalal.com/fr/company-operation.php

182. hsozkult.geschichte.huberlin.de/rezensionen/type=rezbuecher&id=15595&view= pdf

183. alifta.com

184. jesuisraif.ca

185. alifta.com/Fatawa

186. Jacques Godbout, 205. *La vengeance du désert*, in L'Actualité, mars 2014, p. 23.

187. ifancc.org

188. zabihahalal.com/files/news_en/Maple_Lodge_Farms_Zabiha_Halal_Certification _Change_1383593131.pdf

189. zabihahalal.com/fr/process-faq.php

190. en.wikipedia.org/wiki/Fiqh_Council_of_North_America

191. *Compassionate Living*, été 2015, p. 14-15 and see video at maplelodgeharms.ca.

192. Canada's clients are (in order of importance) : Saudi Arabia, Iraq, United Arab Emirates, Iran, Indonesia, Morocco, Algeria, Turkey, Egypt, Malaysia, Tunisia, Kuwait, Lebanon, Jordan, Bahrain, Qatar, Yemen, Syria and Oman. See publications.gc.ca/collections/collection_2011/agr/A74-1-4-2011-fra.pdf

193. agr.gc.ca/eng/industry-markets-and-trade/statistics-and-market-information/by-region/middle-east-and-north-africa/inside-gulf-cooperation-council-gcc-beef-trade/?id=1441717698363#c

194. ici.radio-canada.ca/nouvelles/economie/2011/04/14/012-viande-halal-croissance.shtml

195. lapresse.ca/le-nouvelliste/actualites/201204/18/01-4516565-abattoir-lafrance-vendue.php

196. Nigeria's population is entirely islamized.

197. fuelfix.com/blog/2013/11/10/baker-hugues-africa-leader-finds-solutions-in-shared-knowledge/

198. classiques.uqac.ca/contemporains/helly_denise/enjeux_viande_halal_qc/enjeux_viande_halal_qc.pdf (p. 22)

199. tempsreel.nouvelobs.com/monde/20130214.OBS8961/d-ou-vient-le-cheval-consomme-en-france.html

200. youtube.com/watch?v=o4WddZrR6Ns

201. letemps.ch/suisse/2014/03/12/denner-retire-viande-cheval-rayons

202. Jean-Benoît Nadeau, *La poutine et le kébab*, L'Actualité, mars 2016, p. 41.

203. halalmontreal.com

204. groupexport.ca/fr/repertoire/fiche_entreprise/1128-halal-montreal-certification-authority

205. argent.canoe.ca/nouvelles/affaires/bouffe-halal-agriculteurs-salivent-26102012

206. macnet.ca/English/Pages/About%20MAC.aspx

207. lapresse.ca/actualites/justice-et-affaires-criminelles/affaires-criminelles/201412/01/01-4823948-quelques-anciens-donateurs-du-quebec-au-irfan.php

208. publicsafety.gc.ca/cnt/ntnl-scrt/cntr-trrrsm/lstd-ntts/crrnt-lstd-ntts-eng.aspx#2023

209. pointdebasculecanada.ca/la-mac-qui-englobe-lagence-de-certification-halal-a-contribue-au-collecteur-de-fonds-du-hamas/

210. lapresse.ca/actualites/justice-et-affaires-criminelles/affaires-criminelles/201411/30/01-4823922-dons-au-hamas-une-filiere-tres-active-a-montreal.php

211. pointdebasculecanada.ca/point-de-bascule-repond-directeur-de-information-televisee-radio-canada-jean-pelletier-sur-penetration-services-police-islamistes/

212. viandesgiroux.com/halal [page consulted on January 16, 2015]

213. canadahalalec.com/fromagerie-marie-kade/and canadahalalec.com/les-aliments-karnie/

214. canadahalalec.com/about-us/

215. torontosun.com/2015/03/06/muslim-brotherhood-under-the-microscope-in-canada

216. journaldemontreal.com/2015/01/18/des-mosquees-et-des-ecoles-entre-les-mains-des-islamistes

217. lapresse.ca/la-tribune/sherbrooke/201501/22/01-4837454-le-proprietaire-de-la-mosquee-lie-a-du-financement-juge-louche-par-larc.php

218. AVS is a French association. It made headlines a few years ago because of the very huge penalties it asked from butchers that quitted its ranks. See www.l'express.fr/actualite/societe/religion/l-argent-de-l-islam_497530.html

219. pointdebasculecanada.ca/le-projet-de-conquete-islamique

220. Alec Castonguay, *Le combat de Fatima*, in L'Actualité, mars 2014, p. 18.

221. globalmbwatch.com/2010/12/12/pakistani-newspaper-says-bosnian-grand-mufti-urges-muslims-to-rule-world-through-halal-food

222. fr.wikipedia.org/wiki/Coran

223. fr.wikipedia.org/wiki/Hadith
224. fr.wikipedia.org/wiki/Sunna
225. According to the Koran, "A son's share is twice that of a daughter" (4:12).
226. fr.wikipedia.org/w/index.php?title=Charia
227. On April 2016, New York was the scene of a heated debate on the status of Muslim women under Islamic law. Well known Dutch-Somalian writer and politician Ayaan Hirsi Ali faced off against three other Muslim women and a hostile moderator: "I reject Islamic law because it's totalitarian ... because it's bigoted and especially bigoted against women... Where Islamic law becomes the law of the land ... women will need a male guardian, child marriage is reintroduced, you will be disinherited. If you are raped it's your fault, and you will get stoned to death ... I reject Islamic law because it's inherently hostile to women. It is so bigoted." torontosun.com/2016/04/19/hirsi-ali-shines-in-debate-on-islam
228. islamic-laws.com/taharatandnajasat.htm
229. ici.radio-canada.ca/regions/ontario/2016/04/13/005-aveugles-chiens-toronto-chauffeurs-taxis.shtml
230. fr.muslimvillage.com/2011/03/05/9206/sharia-law-in-australia-already-a-reality/
231. The presence of a shariah-law index at the New York Stock Exchange is all the more surprising when considering that seven US States formally prohibits Islamic Law! See djindexes.com/islamicmarket/
232. lesaffaires.com/mes-finances/placement/tsx--un-nouvel-indice-conforme-etagrave-la-charia-/493945
233. shariahfinancewatch.org/blog/shariah-financial-institutions/
234. tfsa.ca/storage/reports/Canada_Islamic_Finance_2016.pdf
235. euro-jihad.com/blog/?p=4358 [19] fr.wikipedia.org/wiki/D%C3%AEn
236. tfsa.ca/storage/reports/Canada_Islamic_Finance_2016.pdf
237. islamicfinancenews.com/authors/jeffrey-graham,sansvoile.org/2013/12/11/societes-canadien
238. Coopérative d'habitation Qurtuba.
239. On its website, the Islamic Centre of Quebec states that it has officiated 5,000 Islamic wedding ceremonies. See *icqmontreal.com/marriage.html*
240. The *Islamic Centre of Quebec* offers on its website sharia compliant funeral services. It manages the Hamzaz Islamic cemetery located in Laval. See icqmontreal.com/funeral.html. The Association de la sépulture musulmane au Québec also refers to sharia on its website. See sepulturemusulmane.ca/category/lois-et-regles-musulmanes/.
241. Burkini : Swimming wear covering the entire body except face, hands and feet.
242. halalmontreal.com/#!normeshalal/c1wee
243. viandesgiroux.com/halal [page consulted on January 16, 2015]
244. ici.radio-canada.ca/regions/atlantique/2016/01/29/012-abattoir-halal-ile-du-prince-edouard-boeuf-musulmans-acadie.shtml
245. atlanticsignaturebeef.ca/certified-halal-beef-from-atlantic-beef-products/
246. en.wikipedia.org/wiki/Iqbal_Masood_Nadvi
247. ifancc.org/index.php?page=cartifiedcompanies
248. ici.radio-canada.ca/regions/atlantique/2016/03/27/004-acadie-viande-halal-nouveau-brunswick.shtml

249. calgarysun.com/2016/01/24/calgary-muslim-community-holds-food-and-clothing-drive-for-syrian-newcomers-and-the-needy

250. Denise Helly et al., *Les enjeux de la viande halal au Québec*, in *Le halal dans tous ses états* (chap. 6, pp. 101-141), Québec, Les Presses de l'Université Laval, 2014.

251. *Ibid.*

252. journalfa.ca/web/fr/?p=101&id=251

253. *Ibid.*

254. quebec.huffingtonpost.ca/2012/03/13/viande-halal-abattoirdumont_n_1341572.html

255. quebec.huffingtonpost.ca/2012/03/13/viande-halal-abattoirdumont_n_1341572.html

256. *Ibid.*

257. journalexpress.ca/Economie/2010-04-21/article-1272097/Labattoir-Avicomax-bien-present-dans-le-marche-musulman/1

258. sded-drummond.qc.ca/client/page3.asp?page=102

259. affaires.lapresse.ca/portfolio/drummondville/201010/27/01-4336690-nouveau-proprietaire-pour-labattoir-avicomax.ph

260. Félix-Antoine Lorrain, *Halal et rien d'autre*, in Le Devoir, 8 août 2006, p. A4; http://www.assnat.qc.ca/fr/travaux-parlementaires/commissions/capern-39-2/journal-debats/CAPERN-120417.html

261. Denise Helly et al. *Les enjeux de la viande halal au Québec*, in *Le halal dans tous ses états* (chap. 6, pp. 101-141), Québec, Les Presses de l'Université Laval, 2014.

262. lapresse.ca/actualites/national/201106/13/01-4408640-ottawa-songe-a-encadrer-la-certification-halal.php

263. lapresse.ca/le-soleil/affaires/agro-alimentaire/201307/18/01-4672162-mention-halal-facultative-mais-certification-requise.php

264. lapresse.ca/le-soleil/affaires/agro-alimentaire/201307/18/01-4672162-mention-halal-facultative-mais-certification-requise.php

265. inspection.gc.ca/aliments/etiquetage/l-etiquetage-des-aliments-pour-l-industrie/allegations-relatives-a-la-methode-de-production/l-etiquetage-des-produits-alimentaires-halal/fra/1398268634960/1398268807848

266. fr.wikipedia.org/wiki/Christianisme_et_richesse

267. islamfrance.free.fr/aumone.html

268. fr.wikipedia.org/wiki/Imp%C3%B4t_%C3%A0_taux_unique

269. alifta.net/Fatawa/FatawaChapters.aspx?languagename=fr&View=Tree&NodeID=104&PageNo=1&BookID=25

270. az-zakat.fr/les-beneficaires-de-la-zakat-al-mel/les-employes-de-la-zakat.html

271. alifta.net/Fatawa/FatawaChapters.aspx?languagename=fr&View=Tree&NodeID=104&PageNo=1&BookID=25

272. *Ibid.*

273. shariahfinancewatch.org/blog/2013/10/11/why-do-islamic-charities-send-zakat-to-terrorists-because-shariah-says-they-must/

274. alifta.net/Fatawa/FatawaChapters.aspx?languagename=fr&View=Page&PageID=150&PageNo=1&BookID=25

275. thestar.com/news/gta/2011/01/20/muslim_charity_squandered_money_for_poor.html

276. See tfsa.ca/storage/reports/Canada_Islamic_Finance_2016.pdf. In 2021, estimated halal food sales : $1.2 trillion (US).

277. fr.wikipedia.org/wiki/Haram

278. Félix-Antoine Lorrain, *Halal et rien d'autre*, in Le Devoir, 8 août 2006, p. A4.

279. coran-en-ligne.com/Sourate-005-Al-Ma-ida-La-table-servie-francais.html, verset 87

280. "A fatwa is a nonbinding legal opinion on a point of Islamic law (sharia) given by a qualified jurist in response to a question posed by a private individual, judge or government. A jurist issuing fatwas is called a mufti." A fatwa isn't necessarily a condemnation. It is a religious advice that can address various topics: fiscal rules, ritual practices, food etc. See https://en.wikipedia.org/wiki/Fatwa

281. "Fiqh is Islamic jurisprudence. Fiqh is often described as the human understanding of the sharia, that is human understanding of the divine Islamic law as revealed in the Quran and the Sunnah (the teachings and practices of the Islamic prophet Muhammad and His companions). Fiqh expands and develops Shariah through interpretation (ijtihad) of the Quran and Sunnah by Islamic jurists (ulama) and is implemented by the rulings (fatwa) of jurists on questions presented to them. Thus, whereas sharia is considered immutable and infallible by Muslims, fiqh is considered fallible and changeable. Fiqh deals with the observance of rituals, morals and social legislation in Islam as well as political system." https://en.wikipedia.org/wiki/Fiqh

282. For instance, see the fatwas issued by the Grand mufti of Saudi Arabia and the advices of Ayatollah Sistani, a mujtahid issuing his personal interpretations (*ijtihad*) on certain points of Islamic law. The *ijtihad* is the ruling based of his reflexion. sistani.org/english/book/46/2044 and sistani.org/english/book/46/2045.

283. South-African imam Habib Bewley's dissidence towards halal certification is particularly virulent : jumuamosquect.com/khutbas/khutba/archive/2012/january/27/article/khutba-on-halal-certification-fiasco.html

284. https://en.wikipedia.org/wiki/Sunnah

285. Whose main compilations, the *Sahih al-Bukhari* and the *Sahih Muslim*, are considered as mostly or totally authentic by the entire community of Sunni Muslims.

286. saphirnews.com/Florence-Bergeaud-Blackler-Le-marche-du-halal-est-une-invention-marketing_a12176.html; liberation.fr/debats/2017/01/05/florence-bergeaud-blackler-le-halal-est-ne-industriel-fruit-du-neoliberalisme-et-du-fondamentalisme_1539349; ikim.gov.my/new-wp/index.php/2019/09/03/halal-consumerism-as-part-of-halal-ecosystem/

287. Cited in: slate.fr/story/67759/halal-alimentation-viande-livre-turin

288. ''Le verset [5:5 du Coran] selon lequel la viande des Gens du Livre est licite a permis pendant de nombreuses années de consommer ou d'être peu vigilant vis-à-vis de la viande non sacrifiée''. Aujourd'hui, la concurrence internationale privilégie les conceptions plus étroites comme celle de la Malaisie selon le principe de ''qui peut le plus peut le moins'', on garde la méthode qui peut satisfaire les plus exigeants. saphirnews.com/Florence-Bergeaud-Blackler-Le-marche-du-halal-est-une-invention-marketing_a12176.html

289. *Ibid.*

290. lesalonbeige.blogs.com/my_weblog/2011/02/halalisation.html. See also: Florence Bergeaud-Blacker, *Le marché halal ou l'invention d'une tradition*, Seuil, 2017.

291. lalibre.be/economie/actualite/la-certification-halal-est-un-phenomene-de-marketing-51b8bfe5e4b0de6db9bc562e

292. Félix-Antoine Lorrain, *Halal et rien d'autre*, in Le Devoir, 8 août 2006, p. A4.

293. fr.wikipedia.org/wiki/D%C3%AEn

294. http://islam1.org/khutub/Defn_of_Deen_&_Islam.htm

295. *I wonder if anyone will accuse him of being a racist or a bigot for opposing halal certification ?* webcache.googleusercontent.com/search?q=cache:pTwF6-kJRPEJ: pickeringpost.com/story/islamic-scholars-blast-halal-scam/4231+&cd= 1&hl=fr&ct=clnk&gl=ca

296. jumuamosquect.com/khutbas/khutba/archive/2012/january/27/article/khutba-on-halal-certification-fiasco.html

297. halalmontreal.com/#!normeshalal/c1wee

298. foodnewsinternational.com/2014/09/24/europe-cambridge-engineered-solutions-expands-overseas-receives-halal-certification-for-products/#sthash.eRkdHRjy.dpuf

299. francais.islammessage.com/Article.aspx?i=790 [page consulted on January 16, 2015]

300. fr.wikipedia.org/wiki/Bid%60ah

301. Reported by Ahmed, Abou Dawud no 4657 and At-Tirmidhi – authentified by Shaykh Al-Albani in its correction of Sunan Abi Dawud.

302. canadianpackaging.com/features/reinventing-the-veal-march-2015-canadian-packaging/

303. sciencesetavenir.fr/sante/20141020.OBS2612/alcool-viande-de-porc-comment-le-test-halal-les-detecte-t-il.html

304. ''On reconnaît l'intégrisme religieux à sa capacité d'instrumentaliser la religion pour se rapprocher du politique et imposer ses valeurs à l'ensemble de la société, afin que les lois divines aient préséance sur les lois des hommes.'' Louise Mailloux, *La laïcité ça s'impose!*, Les éditions du Renouveau québécois, 2011, p. 85.

305. For instance : Norway, Sweden, Switzerland, Iceland, Denmark and Latvia.

306. cjnews.com/news/kashrut-bodies-seek-greater-co-ordination-federal-inspectors

307. usherbrooke.ca/sodrus/fileadmin/sites/sodrus/documents/Immigration/immigration1 .pdf

308. journalexpress.ca/Economie/2010-04-21/article-1272097/Labattoir-Avicomax-bien-present-dans-le-marche-musulman/1

309. In an open letter dated June 10, 2010 destined to Nicolas Sarkozy, French animal protection groups stress the discriminatory character of these practices : Il nous revient en effet de militer pour une ''objection de conscience'' à la consommation de viande susceptible de provenir d'animaux qui n'ont pas été rendus insensibles à la douleur lors de leur abattage, puisque les motivations éthiques de ceux qui exigent l'insensibilisation des animaux ne sont pas respectées à l'égal des motifs davantage traditionnels que religieux de ceux qui la refusent.

310. ''La liberté de conscience constitue la pierre angulaire de la laïcité. Ce droit stipule que personne ne peut manipuler ou utiliser les lois – ou les chartes – pour brimer de quelque façon que ce soit cette liberté. Se situant au-dessus des croyances particulières, l'État laïque, neutre, protège l'adhésion libre à toutes les croyances dans la mesure où celles-ci ne troublent pas l'ordre public ou n'affectent pas l'intégrité des personnes; de la même façon, il protège la non-croyance. Un État laïque n'est ni athée ni anticlérical, mais il protège autant ceux qui pratiquent une religion que ceux qui n'en pratiquent aucune. En même temps, il n'encourage ni ne soutient ni les uns, ni les autres.'' Source : Coalition Laïcité Québec, laicitequebec.org

311. Nos choix de consommateurs entretiennent une industrie mondiale qui tue chaque année entre 60 et 100 milliards d'animaux terrestres et 1 000 milliards d'animaux marins. « Lorsqu'une société accepte comme allant de soi la pure et simple utilisation d'autres êtres sensibles au service de ses propres fins, n'accordant guère de considération au sort de ceux qu'elle instrumentalise, ses principes moraux sont mis à rude épreuve. » Matthieu Ricard, *Plaidoyer pour les animaux*, Allary Éditions, 2014, p. 89.

312. bbc.com/news/uk-26463064

313. Let us remember the scandals, a few years ago in Quebec, of ducks beaten and kicked in an Eastern township 'foie gras farm' or, in 2014, de atrocious plight of calves captured on hidden camera by *Mercy for Animals* at the Délimax plant of Pont-Rouge, near Quebec City. In the second case, cruelty charges were laid against an employee. The instrumentalization of animals is a concrete incarnation of an anthropocentric vision of the world, intrinsically violent. For instance, the troubling association that the so-called "sport hunters" do between 'rifle' and "being close to nature and fauna". In short, it's the consumers that contribute to perpetuate the system of continuous mass killing of animals.

314. Al-Hafiz Basheer Ahmad Masri, *Les animaux en Islam*, trad. Sébastien Sarméjeanne, préface et relecture scientifique de Malek Chebel, Éditions Droits des animaux, 2014.

315. Harold P. Gastwirt, *Fraud, Corruption, and Holiness: The Controversy Over the Supervision of Jewish Dietary Practice in New York City 1881-1940*, Kennikat Press, Port Washington N.Y. and London, 1974, p. 82-83.

316. people.ucalgary.ca/~elsegal/Shokel/080620_KosherCrime.html

317. animallaw.info/sites/default/files/Journal%20of%20Animal%20Law%202005.01. pdf

318. fr.wikipedia.org/wiki/Moloch

319. newscientist.com/article/dn10712-halalstandard-slaughtering-doesnt-need-animals-awake.html

320. vosizneias.com/98200/2012/01/04/new-york-shechita-wars

321. everything2.com/title/Shechita

322. cor.ca/view/553/why_is_kosher_meat_more_expensive_than_non_kosher_meat. html

323. cjnews.com/news/kashrut-bodies-seek-greater-co-ordination-federal-inspectors

324. Zushe Yosef Blech, *Kosher Food Production*, Ames, Iowa: Blackwell, 2004, p. 187-201.

325. forward.com/articles/1074/glatt-kosher-meat-is-not-all-it-is

326. massorti.com/Le-sens-de-la-Cacherout

327. spectrum.library.concordia.ca/7228/1/Lapidus_PhD_S2011.pdf

328. istitutobioetica.org/Bioetica%20sociale/multiculturalismo/Lerner%20Rabello% 20Macellazione.htm

329. academieveterinaire.free.fr/academie/les%20lois.htm

330. Félix-Antoine Lorrain, *Halal et rien d'autre*, Le Devoir, 8 août 2006, p. A4.

331. classiques.uqac.ca/contemporains/helly_denise/enjeux_viande_halal_qc/enjeux_ viande_halal_qc.pdf, p. 24-25, note 19.

332. In France, the CEOs of the two biggest providers of halal meat, LDC and Zaphir, are respectively of Christian and Jewish confession. See laic.info/2013/08/national/sont-les-dirigeants-des-plus-grandes-entreprises-halal [page consulted on April 21, 2015]

333. saphirnews.com/Florence-Bergeaud-Blackler-Le-marche-du-halal-est-une-invention-marketing_a12176.html

334. cjnews.com/node/83386

335. Sourate 5 (Al-Mâ'ida La table servie):3, translated by Muhammad Hamidullah.

336. fr.wikipedia.org/wiki/Dhabiha

337. Some passages from the hadiths refer to ''honor killings '' such as stoning of adulterous women.

338. fr.wikipedia.org/wiki/Hadith

339. nku.edu/~kenneyr/Islam/Reliance.html

340. la-croix.com/Religion/Actualite/Le-Danemark-interdit-l-abattage-rituel-des-animaux-2014-02-14-1106532

341. amquebec.net/amquebec/images/stories/Documents/memoire_amq.pdf, page 22.

342. vigilancehallal.com/comment-se-pratique-labattage-halal

343. hayat.ca/2012/04/11/labattage-halal-pour-les-nuls

344. en.wikipedia.org/wiki/Wilhelm_Schulze

345. See unstunnedhalal.com/articles/view/?id=22; themodernreligion.com/misc/an/an_slaughter.htm and the website of the Ontarian halal meat company Halal Choice halalchoice.ca/halal.html [pages consulted on January 16, 2015]

346. View his press conference at : https://youtu.be/LiGu_1g9RoM and see also lapresse.ca/le-soleil/affaires/agro-alimentaire/201203/14/01-4505564-le-depute-andre-simard-inquiet-de-labattage-rituel.php

347. ici.radio-canada.ca/nouvelles/Politique/2012/03/15/004-viande-halal-veterinaires-politique-etiquetage.shtml

348. lapresse.ca/le-soleil/affaires/agro-alimentaire/201210/18/01-4584818-abattage-illegal-dagneaux-dans-des-fermes.php

349. lapresse.ca/le-nouvelliste/actualites/201204/18/01-4516565-abattoir-lafrance-vendue.php

350. Among others, youtu.be/Qchz720x9ZU, vimeo.com/51991490, youtu.be/pYnLK-dNP8I, youtu.be/0DP3YtCpS2A

351. For instance, the Islamic Society of North America (ISNA), JAKIM, the Organization of Islamic Cooperation (OIC), the Sheikh Muhammad Al-Najjar of the al-Azhar University and the Islamic World League.

352. halal.gov.my

353. classiques.uqac.ca/contemporains/helly_denise/enjeux_viande_halal_qc/enjeux_viande.html, p. 33.

354. canada.com/montrealgazette/news/business/story.html?id=00582e7f-c6c8-4e29-b620-5d266b141b86&k=4241

355. assnat.qc.ca/Media

356. canada.com/story.html?id=00582e7f-c6c8-4e29-b620-5d266b141b86

357. jumuamosquect.com/khutbas/khutba/archive/2012/january/27/article/khutba-on-halal-certification-fiasco.html

358. francais.islammessage.com

359. *Ibid.*

360. halalmontreal.com/#!normeshalal/c1wee; viandesgiroux.com/halal; lapinduquebec.qc.ca/files/File/etude_sur_le_potentiel_de_marche_du_lapin_certifie_hal al__27_juin_pdf page 9

361. viandesgiroux.com/halal [page consulted on January 16, 2015]

362. laction.com/Actualites/2012-03-27

363. journalexpress.ca/Economie/2010-04-21/article-1272097/Labattoir-Avicomax-bien-present-dans-le-marche-musulman/1

364. giannonepoultry.com/fr/produits/poulet-halal

365. ici.radio-canada.ca/nouvelles/Politique/2012/03/15/004-viande-halal-veterinaires-politique-etiquetage.shtml

366. lapresse.ca/actualites/national/201106/12/01-4408558-produits-halal-en-plein-essor-un-marche-de-632-milliards.php

367. youtube.com/watch?t=10&v=REYTOpeLlFg

368. fil-information.gouv.qc.ca/Pages/Article.aspx?idArticle=2209193900

369. iqra.ca/2012/e-coli-beef-recall-includes-some-halal-products

370. delices-almanar.com/halal.html

371. halalchoice.ca/products.html

372. epicerie-elbaraka.ca/la-signification-du-terme-halal. The Codex Alimentarius Commission was founded in 1961 under the auspices of the United Nations Food and Agriculture Organization (FAO) and the World Health Organization (WHO). It consists of 172 member countries.

373. youtu.be/pYnLK-dNP8I

374. mrctv.org/sites/default/files/embedcache/119743.html

375. youtu.be/nCagJ1ffobg

376. pamelageller.com/wpcontent/uploads/2015/02/ISIS_Slaughtered_21_Christians_in_Libya_18.mp4

377. Including also the ''wild game safaris'' practiced by a certain privileged class who, from Africa to Texas, reproduce the bloodthirsty behavior of the European colonials of the Victorian era.

378. vosizneias.com/98200/2012/01/04/new-york-shechita-wars

379. news.bbc.co.uk/2/hi/uk/2977086.stm

380. bva.co.uk/News-campaigns-and-policy/Newsroom/News-releases/E-petition-to-end-non-stun-slaughter-hits-100 000-as-FSA figures-show-increase-in-non-stun

381. bbc.com/news/uk-26463064

382. tomorrow.is/yesterday/the-time-the-kosher-butcher-was-put-on-trial

383. boucherielawrence.com/blog/les-producteurs

384. tomorrow.is/yesterday/the-time-the-kosher-butcher-was-put-on-trial

385. *Ibid.*

386. peta.org/features/agriprocessors

387. http://gazette.de/Archiv/Gazette-Mai2002/Abattage.html

388. cjnews.com/news/canada/veterinarians-hear-about-kosher-slaughter

389. lhebdodustmaurice.com/%C3%89conomie/Industrie%20agroalimentaire/2012-03-26/article-2939242/Ca-na-rien-a-voir-avec-un-debat-religieux/1

390. cjad.com/CJADLocalNews/entry.aspx?BlogEntryID=10606414

391. chiourim.com/che%E2%80%99hita_%3A_le_bethdin_d%E2%80%99amsterdam_

tape_du_poing_sur_la_table5html

392. See jta.org/2013/08/06/global/french-senator-receives-death-threats-over-anti-shechitah-stance; legrandsoir.info/la-senatrice-udi-goy-chavent-menacee-de-mort-et-accusee-d-antisemitisme-elle-porte-plainte.html. Chilling account made by Ms Goy-Chavent (video in French) at dailymotion.com/video/x17y3ud

393. thenews.pl/1/9/Artykul/121177,Scientists-claim-kosher-and-halal-animal-slaughter-is-inhumane-and-cruel

394. lefigaro.fr/flash-actu/2014/12/10/97001-20141210FILWWW00196-la-pologne-autorise-a-nouveau-l-abattage-rituel.php

395. la-croix.com/Religion/Actualite/Le-Danemark-interdit-l-abattage-rituel-des-animaux-2014-02-14-1106532

396. col.fr/IMG/pdf/animal.pdf

397. col.fr/article-43.html

398. academieveterinaire.free.fr/academie/les%20lois.htm

399. cjnews.com/news/kashrut-bodies-seek-greater-co-ordination-federal-inspectors

400. maplelodgemaltraite.ca

401. zabihahalal.com/fr/process.php

402. journalexpress.ca/Economie/2010-04-21/article-1272097/Labattoir-Avicomax-bien-present-dans-le-marche-musulman/1

403. hebdosregionaux.ca/monteregie/2011/12/17/le-commerce-halal-sinstalle-a-chateauguay

404. isnahalal.ca/info.html

405. delices-almanar.com/halal.htm

406. classiques.uqac.ca/contemporains/helly_denise/enjeux_viande_halal_qc/enjeux_viande.html

407. en.wikipedia.org/wiki/Wilhelm_Schulze

408. unstunnedhalal.com/articles/view/?id=22 [page consulted on January 16, 2015]

409. classiques.uqac.ca/contemporains/helly_denise/enjeux_viande_halal_qc/enjeux_viande. html

410. *Experiments for the objectification of pain and consciousness during conventional (captive bolt stunning) and religiously mandated (ritual cutting) slaughter procedures for sheep and calves. /* The Animal Welfare Act of 24 July 1972 (Tier SchG), by W. Schulze, H. Schultze-Petzold, A.S. Hazem and R. Gross.

411. newscientist.com/article/dn17972-animals-feel-the-pain-of-religious-slaughter.html#.VTBMCX61bZ6

412. themodernreligion.com/misc/an/an_slaughter.htm

413. yasminqureshi.org.uk/about-yasmin

414. unstunnedhalal.com/articles/view/?id=59 [page consulted on January 16, 2015]

415. kosher basel.ch/index

416. peta.org/features/agriprocessors

417. failedmessiah.typepad.com/failed_messiahcom/2004/12/rabbi_dr_im_lev.html

418. *Ibid.*

419. failedmessiah.typepad.com/failed_messiahcom/2004/12/peta_responds_t.html

420. nytimes.com/2017/12/20/us/president-trump-iowa-commutation.html

421. shechitauk.org/fileadmin/user_upload/pdf/Physiological_insights_into_Shechita__S.D.Rosen__Veterinary_Record_2004.pdf; bbc.com/news/magazine-14895534

422. jewishnews.co.uk/scientific-advisor-shechita-uk-opponents-peddle-offensive-falsehoods
423. shechitauk.org/about-us/who-we-are.html
424. shechitauk.org/about-us/testimonials.html
425. foodscience.cals.cornell.edu/people/joe-regenstein [page consulted on January 19, 2015]
426. *Ibid.*
427. *Ibid.*
428. *Ibid.*
429. grandin.com/ritual/kosher.slaugh.html
430. kosjerslachten.nl/wp-content/uploads/2011/05/Preliminary-Report-Regenstein-230511l.pdf
431. jewishvirtuallibrary.org/jsource/judaica/ejud_0002_0009_0_09303.html
432. vosizneias.com/98200/2012/01/04/new-york-shechita-wars
433. upc-online.org/Fall05/grandin.html
434. *Ibid.*
435. forward.com/articles/137318/maximizing-animal-welfare-in-kosher-slaughter
436. kosjerslachten.nl/wp-content/uploads/2011/05/Preliminary-Report-Regenstein-230511l.pdf
437. unstunnedhalal.com/articles/view/?id=22 [page consulted on January 16, 2015]
438. quranandscience.com/quran-science/animals/163-between-the-islamic-method-of-slaying-animals-zabah-halal-a-human-health-abstract
439. thejc.com/print/124319
440. jodendom.online.nl/gfx/artikelen/jodendom/Physiological_insights_into_Shechita_S.D.Rosen_Veterinary_Record_2004_01.pdf
441. jewishnews.co.uk/scientific-advisor-shechita-uk-opponents-peddle-offensive-falsehoods
442. For instance, see the ADL document posted by the Bnai B'rith : col.fr/IMG/pdf/animal.pdf
443. fawc.co.uk/reports/pb8347.pdf
444. Full report available at rituel.jimdo.com/%C3%A9tudes-et-rapports
445. Anil, M.H. et al. 1995. *Welfare of Calves – 2. Increase in Vertebral Artery Blood Flow following Exsanguination by Neck Sticking and Evaluation of Chest Sticking as an Alternative Slaughter Method.* Meat Science, vol .41, 2, 113-123.
446. *Ibid.*
447. Blackmore, D.K. (1984), *Differences in behavior between sheep and calves during slaughter.* Research in Veterinary Science 37, pp. 223-226.
448. Anil, M.H. et coll. 1995. *Welfare of Calves – 2. Increase in Vertebral Artery Blood Flow following Exsanguination by Neck Sticking and Evaluation of Chest Sticking as an Alternative Slaughter Method.* Meat Science, vol 41, 2, 113-123.
449. (Newhook, C. J.; Blackmore, D. K. (1982a) : *Electroencephalographic studies of stunning and slaughter of sheep and calves – Part 2: The onset of permanent insensibility in calves during slaughter.* Meat Science 6, 295-300.
450. Anil et al. 1995b

166

451. Gibson, T.J., Johnson, C.B., Murrel, J.C., Hull, C.M., Mitchinson, S.L., Stafford, K.J., Johnstone, A.C. et Mellor, D.J., 2009a. *Electroencephalographic responses of halothane-anaesthetised calves to slaughter by ventral-neck incision without prior stunning.* New Zealand Veterinary Journal 57(2), 77-83. Gibson, T.J., Johnson C.B., Murrell, J.C., Chambers, J.P., Stafford, K.J. et Mellor, D.J., 2009b. *Components of electroencephalographic responses to slaughter in halothane-anaesthetised calves: Effects of cutting neck tissues compared with major blood vessels.* New Zealand Veterinary Journal 57(2), 84-89.

452. abattagerituel.com/pdf/DP-abattage.pdf

453. *Douleurs animales : les identifier, les comprendre, les limiter chez les animaux d'élevage,* at : cens.nantes.inra.fr/psdr/Altervibio/R31_Leneindre_guatteo_2009.pdf

454. Cited in the comprehensive press file abattagerituel.com/pdf/DP-abattage.pdf

455. issuu.com/florencebergeaud-blackler/docs/coperci_2005

456. newscientist.com/article/dn17972-animals-feel-the-pain-of-religious-slaughter.html

457. al-kanz.org/2008/06/10/halal-abattage-rituel; http://www.kosjerslachten.nl/wp-content/uploads/2011/05/Preliminary-Report-Regenstein-230511l.pdf

458. shechitauk.org/fileadmin/user_upload/pdf/Physiological_insights_into_Shechita_S.D.Rosen_Veterinary_Re cord_2004.pdf

459. lionaid.org/news/2011/09/endorphins-nociceptors-pain-and-fox-hunting.htm

460. Matthieu Ricard, *Plaidoyer pour les animaux,* Allary Éditions, 2014, p. 242, note 36.

461. Kotula, A.W. & Helbacka, N.V. 1966. *Blood Volume of Live Chickens and Influence of Slaughter Technique on Blood Loss.* Poultry Science. 45: 684-688.

462. Kotula, A.W. & Helbacka, N.V 1966. *Blood retained by Chicken Carcasses and cut-up parts as Influenced by Slaughter Methods.* Poultry Science. 45: 404-410.

463. Bywater, H.E. 1968, *Humane Slaughtering of Food Animals – Current Developments; Religious Slaughter.* Vet. Annual 34-41.

464. Blackmore, D.K. 1976. *Effects of Different Slaughter Methods on Bleeding Sheep.* Vet. Rec. 99: 312-316.

465. ncbi.nlm.nih.gov/pubmed/22054488

466. Food Reseach Institute. Biennial Report 1983-85. *Guidelines to Humane Slaughter.*

467. Halil A et Nazl B. (2001) *Studies on the effect of electrical stunning method applied of ante-mortem sheeps on meat quality.* Veteriner-Fakultesi-Dergisi-Istanbul. 27(2): 585-603.

468. ingentaconnect.com/content/ufaw/aw/2004/00000013/00000004/art00001

469. ingentaconnect.com/content/ufaw/aw/2006/00000015/00000004/art00002

470. newscientist.com/article/dn10712-halalstandard-slaughtering-doesnt-need-animals-awake.html#.VTgrVX61bUA

471. eblex.org.uk/wp/wp-content/uploads/2013/04/slaughter_and_meat_quality_feb_2012-final-report.pdf

472. meatinfo.co.uk/news/fullstory.php/aid/17454/Study_finds_similar_blood_levels_in_halal,_schechita_and_ordinary_meats.html Dominic Kennedy, *Test on halal meat destroys argument for ritual slaughter of animals* [archive], in The Times, September 23, 2014. *Animal Slaughter (Religious Methods)* [archive], in Parliament.uk, November 4, 2014; thejc.com/news/uk-news/anti-shechita-tests-rejected-by-campaigners-1.58379

473. Henri Baruk, *Essais sur la médecine hébraïque dans le cadre de l'histoire juive*, Éditions Zikarone, Paris, 1973. rabbinat.qc.ca/nsite/ksr-2.html474.eblex.org.uk/wp/wp-content/uploads/2013/04/slaughter_and_meat_quality_feb_2012-final-report.pdf

475. psychiatrie.histoire.free.fr/lexiq/lex/acroa.htm

476. consoglobe.com/la-viande-halal-est-elle-meilleure-pour-la-sante-cg

477. Gregory, N.G., *Animal Welfare and Meat Science*, 1998, CABI Publishing.

478. news.harvard.edu/gazette/1999/04.22/igf1.story.html; rndsystems.com/cb_detail_objectname_FA00_InsulinLikeGrowthFactor.aspx; drfuhrman.com/library/Animal_protein_IGF-1_colon_cancer.aspx; lanutrition.fr/les-news/un-regime-riche-en-laitages-et-viandes-augmente-le-risque-de-cancer.html; richardbeliveau.org/images/chroniques/R2014-04-07-AVR-067–CompressedSecured.pdf

479. jewishveg.com/francais/ja.html; jewishveg.com/schwartz/should_jews.html; tikkun.org/nextgen/the-planet-saving-mitzvah-why-jews-should-consider-vegetarianism

480. lemondedesreligions.fr/savoir/le-vegetarisme-est-il-halal-21-08-2014-4197_110.php; droitsdesanimaux.net/musulman-vegetarien-se-detourner-dun-regime-a-base-de-viande; islamicconcern.com/default.asp

481. parl.gc.ca/Content/SEN/Committee/372/lega/witn/jewish-f.htm

482. *Ibid.*

483. *Ibid.*

484. *Ibid.*

485. In a 2008 report titled *"Falling Behind: An International Comparison of Canada's Animal Cruelty Legislation"*, the International Fund for Animal Welfare (IFAW) compares the Canadian legal system with those of 14 countries (Austria, Croatia, Great-Britain, Germany, Malaysia, New-Zealand, Norway, Philippines, Poland, Portugal, South-Africa, Switzerland and Ukraine). The final conclusion will surprise you: under all established criteria Canada is systematically among the last on the list. ifaw.org/canada/resource-centre/falling-behind-international-comparison-canada%E2%80%99s-animal-cruelty-legislation.

486. laws-lois.justice.gc.ca/fra/loisAnnuelles/2008_12/page-1.html

487. *Ibid.*

488. coteboudreau.com/2014/01/18/exploitation-animale-loi

489. "Video auditing is now being used in many large, conventional slaughter plants. Unfortunately, all kosher plants have resisted video auditing. Kosher slaughter of cattle requires special care. While some kosher plants have done well, and many others are improving, too often kosher plants have been very badly managed compared to many of the big conventional plants. In order to maximize animal welfare, kosher slaughterhouses need to take the following steps [...] use video auditing by an outside firm, and practice transparency by streaming the video to a webpage so that the public can view it." forward.com/articles/137318/maximizing-animal-welfare-in-kosher-slaughter/

490. Testimony by Alex Alexiev, Senior Fellow, Center for Security Policy, U.S. Senate Subcommittee on Terrorism, Technology and Homeland Security, June 26, 2003. centerforsecuritypolicy.org/2003/06/26/alexiev-testifies-on-wahhabi-influence-in-us-2/

491. qf.org.qa/about/about

492. mcgill.ca/research/researchers/funding/international/qatar-national-research-fund

493. pointdebasculecanada.ca/participation-de-jacques-fremont-aux-activites-de-la-qatar-fondation-en-2009-rappel-des-positions-totalitaires-de-youssef-qaradawi-le-principal-ideologue-islamiste-soutenu-par-cette-fondati/, spiegel.de/international/world/islam-s-spiritual-dear-abby-the-voice-of-egypt-s-muslim-brotherhood-a-745526.html

494. quebec.huffingtonpost.ca/claude-simard/les-relations-de-luniversite-mcgill-avec-la-dictature-esclavagiste-du-qatar_b_5404250.html

495. archive.is/5eK6c et http://www.tvanouvelles.ca/2015/02/09/une-ecole-privee-financee-par-le-gouvernement-du-koweit

496. kaiciid.org/who-we-are/our-partners

497. berkleycenter.georgetown.edu/cornerstone/saudi-arabia-executes-a-sheikh-and-exacerbates-religious-intolerance, clarionproject.org/analysis/saudi-arabias-interfaith-hypocrisy

498. gatestoneinstitute.org/5194/austria-saudi-kaiciid

499. lapresse.ca/actualites/201109/08/01-4432545-une-charte-des-droits-des-religions.php

500. nice-provence.info/blog/2016/04/15/freres-musulmans-tariq-ramadan-hani-ramadan-nice/

501. pointdebasculecanada.ca/colloque-sur-le-halal-a-montreal-subventionne-par-des-institutions-publiques-participation-de-tariq-ramadan/

502. pointdebasculecanada.ca/programme-et-participants-au-colloque-le-halal-dans-tous-ses-etats/

503. https://sencanada.ca/en/Content/Sen/committee/412/secd/51823-e

504 ottawacitizen.com/news/politics/foreign-donations-to-foster-extremist-ideology-fly-under-canadas-radar

505. telegraph.co.uk/news/worldnews/middleeast/iraq/11140860/Qatar-and-Saudi-Arabia-have-ignited-time-bomb-by-funding-global-spread-of-radical-Islam.html

506. Namely, about 6% of the world's oil reserves and 40% of those of gas.

507. Nafeez Mosaddeq Ahmed, *America and the Taliban: From Co-operation to War*, Global Dialogue volume 4, number 2, Spring 2002, *The Impact of 11 September.*

508. Ahmed Rashid, *The Taliban: Exporting Extremism*, Foreign Affairs 78, no 6 (November/December 1999), p. 31.

509. Nafeez Mosaddeq Ahmed, *America and the Taliban: From Co-operation to War,* Global Dialogue volume 4, number 2, Spring 2002, The Impact of 11 September.

510. Ahmed Rashid, *Taliban: Militant Islam, Oil and Fundamentalism in Central Asia* (New Haven, Conn.: Yale University Press, 2000), p. 201.

511. *Taleban in Texas for Talks on Gas Pipeline*, BBC News, 4 décembre 1997.

512. Speech of Congressman Dana Rohrabacher, *US Policy toward Afghanistan*, Senate Foreign Relations Subcommittee on South Asia, 14 avril 1999.

513. Nafeez Mosaddeq Ahmed, *America and the Taliban: From Co-operation to War*, Global Dialogue volume 4, number 2, Spring 2002, *The Impact of 11 September.*

514. *Afghan Women Warn against the Northern Alliance*, Institute for Public Accuracy news release, November 15, 2001 [accuracy.org/press_releases/PR111501.htm].

515. worlddialogue.org/content.php?id=200

516. "Friend", meaning "backed by the United-States during the Iran-Iraq War of 1980-1988"... A country that was also simultaneously selling armament to Iran. In 1987, the

revelation of those *secret sales* became the Irangate scandal. Hussein became *an enemy* upon the August 1990 invasion of Kuwait (that lead to the Gulf War).

517. washingtonsblog.com/2016/02/terrorists-arent-hitting-u-s-now.html

518. For instance, the secular, multi-faith Syria of Bachar Al-Assad.

519. tunisiefocus.com/politique/interventions-militaires-etats-unis-ont-abouti-renforcement-terrorisme-148641/

520. lepoint.fr/actualites-chroniques/2007-01-17/le-maitre-a-penser-de-l-islamisme-radical/989/0/30921

522. gov.uk/government/publications/muslim-brotherhood-review-main-findings

523. isna.ca/3/114/isna-canada-welcomes-the-election-of-justin-trudeau youtu.be/aliEvkTigu4

524. Speaking of inequality : While in 2016 the Residential and long-term care centers (CHSLDS) allowed barely $2.17 for each elderly meal, Quebec prisons allotted $6.98 for every kosher meal and $4.10 for every halal meal served to prisoners. journaldequebec.com/2016/06/29/a-peine-217-par-repas-en-chsld; lapresse.ca/actualites/201607/22/01-5003796-le-cout-de-la-diete-religieuse-bondit-dans-les-prisons.php

525. lesoir.be/1417467/article/actualite/belgique/2017-01-16/wallonie-l-abattage-sans-etourdissement-bientot-int